HEALER:

REDUCING CRISES

ELIZABETH POWER, M.Ed.

EPower & Associates, Inc. | Nashville, TN

Published and distributed by EPower & Associates, Inc. Nashville TN (epowerandassociates.com and elizabethpower.com)

Cover design: Clarice Barrington
Edited by Wendy H. Jones
Interior design: Amit Dey

Library of Congress Cataloging-in-Publication Data

Library of Congress Control Number 2021902029
Paperback ISBN: 978-1-883307-03-5

1ˢᵗ Edition, February 2021

PRAISE FOR HEALER: REDUCING CRISES

"This book is a must-read for anyone who has experienced trauma of any kind or knows someone who has. Whether an action taken against them or an event witnessed, they'll benefit from looking at it from Elizabeth Power's perspective.

"Written with her depth of insight into the world of trauma and her unfailing ability to make complicated subject matter understandable, she has made available unique resources both in the book and online to help therapists, counselors, and those striving to recover from the effects of trauma.

"Reading this could change your life and/or give you the skills and information needed to help someone else change theirs for the better... has had a profound effect on my life; I can't wait to see what the next book will offer!"

— **Ann Coward, JD, MCSP,** GradDip. Phys.

"Elizabeth Power is a brilliant, trusted, accomplished Healer. Her book reflects her broad knowledge and provides concrete approaches to reducing the impact of crises and trauma to build a more rewarding life. Easy to read and use, this book is for everyone. Don't miss it!"

— **Barbara W. Boat, Ph.D.,** University of Cincinnati

TABLE OF CONTENTS

FOREWORD

I feel extremely fortunate to know Elizabeth Power and humbled that she has asked me to write this foreword to *Healer*. Quite possibly you will never have the chance to meet her in person. But the pages that follow vividly convey a very good idea of what a wise and wonderful soul she is.

Elizabeth and I come from very different places, geographically, culturally, and professionally. She "came up" in Appalachia. I was "reared" in New Yawk City. My heritage is Jewish. Her religious affiliation is Episcopalian. I am a licensed psychotherapist and have spent the great majority of my adult life as an academic.

She has worn many hats, but much of her work has been in the business sector. Elizabeth has aligned with many cultures and sub-cultures, living and working among corporate types, staunchly conservative inhabitants of small towns, ever-so "sophisticated" residents of major cities, and indigenous communities in various parts of the world.

My life experiences have been diverse, but nowhere near as diverse as hers. Yet, ultimately, we are kindred spirits. Neither of us is in the habit of marching down Main Street, although I certainly live a more routine existence than she does.

What we do share, besides the joy of rapid repartee and a wicked sense of humor, is a belief in the basic competency of people and a disdain for a mental health "industry" that requires people seeking help to be labeled as being deficient in one way or another to receive that help.

Despite years of doctoral-level training in clinical psychology and decades as a university professor who trained clinical psychologists, I have never subscribed to the prevailing view of what leads people into therapists' offices. And, Lord knows, neither has Elizabeth.

The belief we share is that although the sources of distress that people encounter can interfere with their ability to function, the opposite is true as well. Unpreparedness to function as an autonomous adult – at home, at work, at school, with one's family, in the larger community – can foster anxiety, depression, substance abuse, any number of other psychological difficulties – including, practically inevitably, low self-esteem.

None of us is fortunate enough to have mastered the full range of abilities needed to navigate all the many situations we encounter as we make our way through life. Too many of us lack a large swath of these capacities. For one reason or another, we simply didn't have access to the opportunities that would have endowed us with these skills.

Many people – people who have lived through trauma, the people in their lives, and professionals who strive to help them – believe that overcoming the horrors of trauma is all about revisiting nightmarish events and facing those horrors all over again.

Elizabeth knows better, largely from hard-won, first-hand experience. Although at some point confronting past traumas may be helpful or even necessary to move forward, what survivors of trauma need first and foremost, especially if much of their trauma occurred in childhood, is to be fortified by mastering the life skills that should have been transmitted to them in their formative years but for one reason or another were not.

This book and the others in the series cover the territory that Elizabeth and I believe is essential to begin absorbing the capacities needed to overcome the exhausting effects of trauma and live a rich, fulfilling life. If that idea sounds unfamiliar... hell even if it doesn't... turn the page and prepare yourself for an enlightening and uplifting journey.

Steven N. Gold, PhD

Licensed Clinical Psychologist

Past President,

American Psychological Association Division 56 Trauma

Editor in Chief, APA *Handbook of Trauma Psychology*

Author, *Contextual Trauma Therapy* and *Not Trauma Alone*

1

EXPAND YOUR CAPACITIES

Overview

Why is this the first book in the series? Simple: the importance of its content. While it's true that you can complete the series in any order, this first volume holds the most basic skills. Everyone has some of these skills, and everyone needs more.

I sat with Don (not Don's actual name) last week, a fellow I'd worked around in a corporate environment a long time ago. "How are you and yours making out with all this isolation? Everybody healthy in your world?" I asked him.

"Yeah, we're all still on this side of the grave," he laughed. "It's tough, but if we hadn't had all that soft-skills training, that ooshy stuff you teach, it'd be worse."

"Like what?" I challenged him. "What in particular?"

"Oh," he said, "I always thought I was "just a" line worker, and when we looked at what it really took, I felt a lot prouder of me. And I could feel it. That's that stuff you teach about strengths."

"What'd you do with it?" I asked.

"Well, I taught myself German on the sly—I didn't tell anyone I was doing it. And the wife and I saved up a pile of money and went to Germany for a couple of months around the change-over shut down. "Imagine her surprise when I could communicate with everybody we needed to. Almost didn't come back," he said. "But we did. And when we came back? I just started translating engineering drawings and parts and tool information. Turned out to be a big help. Now I tutor high school kids!" I could see his pride.

Sometimes we just need more information and a few different tools. As you practice, you strengthen your skill and stamina in these four areas. It becomes more difficult for life to "bowl you over." It becomes easier to create and support sturdier relationships.

I hope you buy into defining trauma based on how it impacts you rather than on an event's name. Considering that impact-based definition, these are the four foundational sets of knowledge and skills everyone needs to sharpen and strengthen:

Elastic Emotions: the ability to identify, assess, and turn feelings up and down in volume in different circumstances. Being able to regulate your emotions creates choice, and choice is fundamental in power. Overwhelming negative experiences deprive people of options and stall emotional development. They make people feel powerless. When traumatic experiences occur in childhood, people miss the opportunity to learn about their emotions and the tools for handling them. They miss the most fundamental choices others have in situations where things are "good enough." Every choice and option you can identify and master restores a bit of your ability to have power in your world.

Every emotion—and feeling—you can identify, and master helps you manage its volume. This decreases the territory your negative emotions occupy. Of course, you still feel them, and you have increased the ones you have befriended. These outcomes counter the impact of trauma.

Finding Connections. This the skill of recognizing different kinds of connections and knowing how to use them for self-soothing. We do a lot of this naturally without realizing it. We hear a song and think of someone. We glance down and see a piece of jewelry someone gave us and think of them.

Because we are generally not aware of the connections, we miss the power they have. Those positive connections can and do help us. We're much more familiar with brain-hijacking negative connections.

We have negative connections—triggers—and we get upset when these gnarly reminders pop up. With an awareness of our choices and lots of practice, we can create more reminders (triggers) that are pleasant.

Overwhelming experiences enhance and strengthen the negative because the brain's job is to keep us safe. We can help our brains bathe in the feel-good chemicals at will. Good, positive connections support learning the proper use of power. They help develop empathy and are soothing.

Repossessing Life: all too often, we give our lives over to our history or a specific difficulty. Taking our lives back is critical. If the only focus we have is a painful history, we miss a whole dimension of investments we might make in our future.

Secret Strengths: one of the missing elements for many who have checkered pasts or who deal with crappy stuff in the present is recognition of strengths. Consider the lens through which you look at your behavior and choices. By now, you can tell there's a difference in this book's perspective. To keep building on that, invest in downloadable learning based on this book.

The relationship of this content to your success

The knowledge we offer and the skills you choose to develop help you accomplish at least two critical tasks.

First, the knowledge and skills help you improve your "EQ" – the measure of your Emotional Intelligence. EQ skills (self-awareness, self-regulation, social awareness, relationship skills, and empathy) are the ones that help you advance in your career and are vital parts of success. Current thinking is that EQ is an essential element for success in your job.

Your EQ is an extension of skills acquired in childhood called SEL. SEL stands for Social-Emotional Learning. Many people develop SEL skills at home when things at home are good enough (not perfect). In different cultures, the way these qualities or skills are taught and expressed varies based on the culture. SEL skills are the same skills as those that make up your EQ in adulthood.

Second, this same skill set helps you master traumatic experiences by developing healthy insulation against trauma's consequences. In particular, and for this volume, self-awareness and self-regulation are key. Trauma, especially in childhood, derails our efforts to develop self-regulation. Children may even become mute, as Maya Angelou did, to preserve their safety. Symbolically, becoming mute is an extreme form of isolation, which is another typical response to trauma.

When (or if) you begin to see a therapist, these skills make your work easier. They'll make the therapist's job easier too. In your work life, you'll find yourself able to stay calmer, respond more effectively, and feel less stressed. Of course, they can't compensate for truly toxic environments, but they can help you in difficult situations until you choose to better your circumstances.

In other words, there's just about no way that this knowledge or these skills are harmful—unless you choose to use them to bully others. Then we'll need to talk about power.

About the series

This book is the first in a series with expanded content from The Trauma-Informed Academy (TIA). It includes the Trauma-Responsive System (TRS), which focuses on action and simple skill development and values that promote positive relationships such as community, collaboration, and reciprocity.

Every book in this series acknowledges that all trauma is change and that not all change is traumatic. Every book in this series recognizes that we have more in common than we do differences.

You can read the series in any order. What matters the most is that you read it and wear it to see how it can support you. Practice is also critical.

Each book in the series focuses on a grouping of skills—ways of thinking, feeling, and acting. Sometimes these are skills our environment couldn't help us learn. Sometimes we were too overwhelmed to master them. Sometimes we find ourselves at a place in life where increasing them would be helpful. These skills are part of talent development, training departments, personal and professional development. Learn them here to make sure that they include an understanding of trauma that is helpful, non-pathologizing, and adds value to your life.

For whom is this written?

We recognize that a wide variety of experiences in the workplace, at home, in faith communities, with friends, in every situation can overwhelm us to the point that it's hard to make sense of things.

We know they occur across the lifespan and that there are many reasons people are sometimes more vulnerable in some situations than in others. We know that whatever development children attain as they reach maturity is what they take into the workplace and adult relationships.

Frankly, we all need all the chops or skills we can muster in these challenging times. Whether you are a CEO, an educator, clinician, clergy, or working at home as an entrepreneur—or maybe a student, or retired, boosting your skills is a good thing.

Limits

We expect people to differentiate among experiences that they call upsetting, annoying, distressing, and overwhelming or traumatic. If you are unfamiliar with these differences, we'll help you learn how to figure them out. We also expect that you know when you are giving it your best and still need more to seek counseling.

We expect that the people who read these books and use the accompanying journals will manage their thoughts, feelings, and actions.

As in every book that touches on personal development, remember that threatening to kill yourself or others is a pretty good sign you need more help than we offer. If you feel desperate, call your local emergency system and ask for help.

Next steps

If you want to increase your skills even more, the next step is the video/download course that walks you through these. Go to elizabethpower.com, click on Training, and then on Trauma to learn more about offerings.

Or maybe you know you're interested in our coaching and training? Your next step is to go to elizabethpower.com and select Get Started. It will walk you through the process of setting up a call.

2

FOUNDATION:
AN IMPACT BASED DEFINITION

Overview

Whatever brings you to this book, whether it's about something at home, inside you, or at work, definitions matter. How you define yourself defines your world.

Suppose you're in the workplace and experiencing some form of gaslighting, harassment, or intimidation. This is for you, too.

In this series, we use specific definitions. Let's look at the foundation for all of them.

How trauma took on two meanings

Terrible things have always happened—and we have thought about them in different ways. Sometimes we've said, "It's the Divine, punishing us." What you believe about this is dependent entirely on your religious or spiritual traditions. Or we say, "That's just the way things were." Sometimes we've made people who experience terrible Things that make us heroes or victims. They may be both or either or neither. Terrible things—traumatic events—have happened since the dawn of time.

Trauma comes from the Greek word spelled the same way. It means wound or injury. Until the late 1800s, trauma referred to only one thing: terrible physical injuries. In the late 1800s, people in Sigmund Freud's world began to talk about injuries that made people hysterical (not as in laughter) as injured by something that happened in childhood. This idea died out only to resurface during World War I.

There was no clarification for the multiple meanings until the 1970s. People who treated gunshot wounds, dramatic physical injuries of all sorts, and the consequences of motor vehicle accidents knew what trauma was: they saw it every day in their surgeries, hospitals, and in the environments where these significant injuries occurred.

In the 1970s, it became clearer that the word **trauma** had two meanings. The difference, simply put, focuses on these two definitions:

- Severe physical injury to the body (how Emergency Rooms and hospitals think of trauma)
- Childhood maltreatment and violence against women (how mental health and social services professionals identified trauma)

Every medical professional who works in the Emergency Rooms knows what trauma is. Their training teaches them that it is a form of major physical injury to the body—like a gunshot wound or injuries from an accident of some sort. Trauma to the body was the focal point, with standardized levels defined in 1976.

This other kind? For soldiers (not first responders), phrases like shell shock, soldier's heart, combat fatigue, and war neurosis were the labels applied to their experiences. The thousand-yard stare of detachment or dissociation after experiencing combat goes as far back as Sophocles' play *Ajax*.

If you are old enough to remember, we only began to talk about childhood maltreatment as a problem in the 1960s. It was 1962 when the American Medical Association's journal published an article that added child abuse to the list of diagnosable medical conditions.

Federal legislation in 1974, the Child Abuse Prevention and Treatment Act (CAPTA), was passed by Congress, dramatically increasing the visibility of trauma as we then identified it: child abuse and neglect.

It was then that mandatory reporting laws existed in every state. "If you see something, say something" isn't a new mantra that the United States created (although it is a great marketing phrase) after the terrorist attacks of 9/11. It's the backbone of legally required reporting of injury to children and other vulnerable populations.

Issues of violence against women also began to be of concern in the 1970s, with the earliest rape crisis centers set up in the early 1970s. I was lucky enough to work with Ann Burgess, DNSc, APRN, FAAN, on the first training grant ever awarded to develop training for people working with sexually assaulted women.

Dr. Burgess was the researcher who defined Rape Trauma Syndrome, a collection of reactions to an overwhelming and horrific event. I met her in my position as the Executive Director of the North Carolina Rape Crisis Association in the last half of the 1970s. The NCRCA was the group awarded the grant to write the training. She supervised our project.

It was a remarkable experience to work with this pioneer in women's issues who was also a forerunner of the trauma-informed movement: she talked about the consequences of what happened as first and foremost in women's mental health.

Domestic Violence became an issue in the same era, even though it would be 1994 before Congress passed the Violence Against

Women Act (VAWA). In 2020, Intimate Partner Violence (IPV, to accommodate men, women, and relationships of all sorts) was the current name for any form (physical, mental, emotional, sexual, financial, or otherwise) of violence in relationships.

Over time, the issue of maltreatment in a larger sense, including harassment, gaslighting, bullying, and more—along with the impact of **other** overwhelming experiences—began to be of concern to all aspects of society.

Now? The impact of overwhelming experiences (forms of psychological trauma) is significant enough that some states legislate Trauma-Informed Care. It is becoming a standard of care.

The limitation is that Trauma-Informed Care focuses on care for injured individuals instead of the social change necessary to change systems that are injurious. We need the next step, Trauma-Responsive Systems, or systems that reduce the risk of experiencing overwhelming events. We'll need to chisel away at change for a long time in systems that support continued traumatization.

Here at **The Trauma-Informed Academy,** we see the impact of overwhelming (traumatic) experiences at home, school, work, medical and faith communities, and anywhere there are people.

We can't exclude pets. People who are abolitionist vegans include animals used for food. We are just learning how trees and plants convey danger, experience loss, and react visibly to injury.

For our focus, we'll confine this work to people (and encourage you to think about it as it applies to your pets, too), although we need to be respectful of all life. We'll work on creating Trauma-Responsive Systems and lifestyles that help people create and sustain sturdy relationships.

Media influence on naming and claiming

The media knows that the best way to increase viewers is to create action and suspense using drama, shock, and surprise. What better to do this than **both** types of traumatic experiences?

The increase in the use of physical (injury to the body) and psychological_trauma (the impact of maltreatment, interpersonal violence, and other catastrophic events) in the media has been steady and exponential.

The fact that *ER* (a television show based on a hospital emergency room) ran 19 seasons, and *Special Victims' Unit*, or *SVU* (another television show about a sex crime unit), ran 20 seasons is part of the evidence about the impact of media on violence and vice versa.

Twenty years. Twenty years of seat-gripping, adrenaline-rushing, gory emergency room stories. People who end up in a hospital emergency room are usually there because of a physical situation—injury or illness—that is overwhelming.

A hospital trip may or may not occur because of some form of assault or injury. The person may or may not call Law Enforcement. Nonetheless, there is apparent victimization and psychological trauma. That experience comes with no guarantee for future justice or legal restoration.

The Simpsons, a TV show known for snarky characters, was a staple of television since 1989 (for 30 seasons). *The Simpsons* was a satire or a parody. Yet, the show may be a defining influence on the rudeness of customer service. Customer service agents and retail sales clerks, who grew up seeing the model of the Simpsons' communication style as acceptable and helpful in society, miss the fact that it is a model for dysfunctional families. The show made the borderline rudeness, ridicule, and general meanness it portrays acceptable if through no other mechanism other than the repetition and acceptance by viewers. The normalization of this communication style via modeling for over 650 episodes has an impact.

According to a recent study conducted by the American Academy of Family Physicians (AAFP), which you can find by searching for AAFP media-violence-entertainment, an average American youth will see 200,000 violent acts on television before age 18. Those same youth average about 13 hours a week playing video games, many of which glorify violence, crimes against people and animals and allow children and youth to practice being perpetrators.

In that study, eighty-one percent of violent scenes in music videos were sexual, sometimes linking beautiful scenery with grotesque violence against women and minorities. Other studies have shown that rap, a newer genre, contains more violence than different music genres.

Further, viewers were more likely to accept the use of violence, violence against women, and to commit violent or aggressive acts themselves. If there is a correlation, we need to figure out how to increase the non-traumatizing content to see if we can shift society in that direction, too.

If your life has been filled with bullying, or emotional, physical, or sexual violence, this kind of content may be more familiar to you and seem more acceptable. It's a common theme in entertainment. The frequency with which we encounter it makes it seem more ordinary.

Geordie was a fabulous dancer with extensive training in ballet and modern dance. She came to the conservatory to increase her abilities and capitalize on her natural talent. One evening she confided that her father used to beat her every time she made a mistake to "toughen her up" for the competitive world of dance. Geordie confessed that when she had a challenging class, one where Geordie didn't feel she performed well, she would smack her feet with heavy books to toughen her up for the pain dancing caused and drive herself to perform better.

You may know people who had these experiences and ended up in relationships where the same behavior occurs. It's what they know. What kind of mate might Geordie seek out if what she knows as motivation is punishment? How might she handle relational errors in other dance companies?

What if you're working on building a life that is more peaceful inside and out? What if you want to have less drama and lower the impact of traumatic experiences in your life? Continued exposure to violent media—television, games, and music—won't help you achieve that goal. Violence against yourself in whatever form slows down your growth, too.

All of this is important—and it misses something critical. It ignores the fact that sometimes the things that influence or overwhelm us may not be overtly awful. Those things may be annoying, irritating, distressing, upsetting, or gnaw at us from the inside out. Those "hidden events" that don't seem so big are another reason to consider impact over event name. They're also a reason to look at the modeling to which we expose ourselves.

Shifts caused by an impact-based definition

So far, all we've talked about is events by name, the things that happen to us. We hyper-focus on one type because of where we are in history or the sociology of a situation. We exclude some, and we push aside others. We decide that some are more significant than others (for example, combat gets a more robust response than domestic violence).

We set up power structures that say "your experience counts; yours doesn't" because we believe what happened to one person is more important than what happened to another. You know: different rules for different people.

This (different rules for different people) influences the persistent public commentary about supporting veterans who develop

PTSD and first responders who develop PTSD. People who survive childhood and relational trauma—women in particular—are not honored, celebrated, supported in the same way. I look forward to future change, where healing is equally crucial for the most disenfranchised groups as it is for the majority group.

Personally? I was diagnosed with PTSD about as soon as it hit the DSM (Diagnostic and Statistical Manual of Mental Disorders) in the early 1980s. The exclusion of trauma as a cause and the selective acceptance of specific diagnoses by groups like NAMI (the National Alliance for the Mentally Ill and any other organization that focuses on biological brain disorders) hinders support and healing.

My brain isn't (wasn't?) the problem. The experiences that shaped ways of thinking, feeling, and being were the problem. The forms of being and doing that I learned were too far outside the norm and made people (and sometimes me) uncomfortable. Yes, they shaped my brain, but the problem originated from what happened to me and its impact. Those events changed me in my entirety. The good news is that I can and have changed myself again (at least a time or two!).

Let's tip the equation. If we move <u>from</u> an event name to an impact-based concept of trauma, what happens?

First, it reduces the power dynamic. In an event-name model, the worse the event, the greater the status assigned. You might hear people say, "Oh, that's not bad… let me tell you what happened to me!" or it could sound like a competition for a prize. An important question is this: who decides what's worse?

"Well," Anna said, "I got hit three times, so that's worse than what happened to you! And when he hit me, I went clear across the room. He broke my nose, my glasses, and my favorite lamp."

"No, it's not, 'cause I got…" LeQuan replied, and they're off and running, competing for who can name and claim how many natural disasters, accidents, medical crises, instances of victimization by crime or relationship. Whoever has the highest count of the events deemed the worst? <u>They</u> win. It's the Olympics of trauma: whoever can tolerate the greatest number of awful things gets the medal. That doesn't make much sense when you think about it.

I hear this in the workplace, too. When people are being harassed and gaslighted, it's easy to point to individual behavior. We can say, "There! He (or she) did that to me! That [insert job title or person's name] is a real piece of work, a psycho..." the issues are systemic and structural, embedded in organizational culture.

In service delivery systems, the person with the diagnosis in the **least** powerful position. Yet this person generates the income stream for the provider. For example, you might hear a provider talk about how many more diagnoses they need to make their monthly revenues. Even if they don't get to the level of "how many of what diagnoses" in their client load, clinics can't stay open without patients. "Sick" people are required to pay the bills.

This unavoidable economic twist brings power to the forefront: who has the diagnosis, how it gets assigned, and who can assume or develop diagnoses? These are critical systems issues focused on power and its use. They involve the power delegated to people who diagnose, people who process records and invoices, people who decide what to pay, and the institutions that get billed.

The current model makes illness and suffering a source of income rather than rewarding healing and strengths. Power differentials that have endured centuries determine whose event matters and whose doesn't.

Second, adopting an impact-based perspective <u>allows for diverse and inclusive experiences</u>. Only specific types of impact can make something traumatic. If a person experiences those types of results, the event is traumatic. Arguing about whose trauma is worse or more numerous is less necessary when considering impact—even though people can compete for that too! An impact-based focus also makes trauma a subjective experience. That event that was over the top for you may have had a minor impact on me.

Every definition of trauma by the organizations that believe they own the right to define it refers to an <u>event</u> that causes a person to have great fear for their lives or sanity or of horrific injury. These organizations include the World Health Organization (WHO) that publishes the International Classification of Diseases (ICD-11) and the Diagnostic and Statistical Manual of Mental Disorders (DSM). The American Psychiatric Association (the APA) publishes the DSM. Frankly, all of us who believe in this work would love to own the definition, and many of us have adapted it to suit our philosophy and structure.

Here at the TIA, we adopted several key stakes that we think are solid. We believe these positions help reduce the impact of overwhelming experiences and the costs we all incur because of them. These "stakes" are:

- Everyone has either seen, heard, or experienced events that have overwhelmed their capacity to respond, even momentarily.

- Each person responds differently to their experiences.

- Everyone benefits from expanding specific skills without regard for their history.

And we ask, "What would happen if we asked how a person was changed by what happened?" They might say, "I felt overwhelmed... I was terrified... I thought I was going to die... there was no way I could make sense of what happened." When you hear these phrases, the event was traumatic. If they say, "It was hard, and I learned a lot," then they have grown from what happened – and if it was traumatic, they hope to be able to end up saying, "it was hard, and I learned a lot."

And in case you missed it, it removes competition for who in a group was the most victimized. Could the same event impact two people very differently? Yes. Suddenly, no matter the name of the event, it's the impact that makes it traumatic.

Trauma is subjective

Listen, here's the challenge—each one of us interprets what happens to us through the lens of our age, vulnerabilities, culture, expectations, strengths, and context. Fireworks may be exciting and wonderful for some and send others right to their closet.

In some cultures, people who hear voices, see things, and live outside of the rest of their peers' everyday reality are considered "healers being born." Dr. Malidoma Patrice Somé teaches that mental disorders are spiritual emergencies. His people, the Dagara, regard these as "good news from the other world."

Dr. Somé holds three Master's degrees and two doctoral degrees from the Sorbonne and Brandeis University. He is a brilliant thinker. *Of Water and the Spirit* chronicles his journey of separation from and restoration to his people. He is an initiated elder in his village in Dano, Burkina Faso, W. Africa. Others echo his beliefs.

Our **reactions** to every event are subjective. They are ours alone and belong to no one else. We interpret everything through what we believe, what our ancestors have taught us, and what frightens or reassures us.

Some of the skills and knowledge that influence how we interpret events are the same as those in Emotional Intelligence. The skills in Emotional Intelligence (measured as EQ) are impaired by being overwhelmed or frightened.

Staying alive in traumatic situations is all about the physical body at the expense of developing ability in Self-Awareness, Self-Regulation, Social Awareness, Social Skills, and

Empathy. The impairment in these areas is the "impact" part of the impact-based definition.

The work based on Daniel Goleman's ideas has shown that Emotional Intelligence (EQ) may be more important than IQ in your career and relationships. The ability to regulate feelings is critical in all relationships, and relationship skills are vital to positive success however you define it. Cultures may develop these skills in different ways.

These are the same skills taught to children in some schools as Social-Emotional Learning. Frankly, the hope is that children can learn these at home—and, if they're not able to because their caregivers don't have these skills, how might we support adults in learning them so that we can upskill generations to come quickly? And how might we support cultures in their methods for helping children learn these?

How do you think everyone's work would be if children and adults had higher levels of these skills? How would the world be different if teachers, faith leaders, social workers, nurses, care-givers in residential facilities, and counselors had measurably higher EQs? Imagine the positive impact it might have. Can you think of any harmful or undesirable consequences?

If, like me, you can only see good from having more skills in self-awareness, self-regulation, social awareness, social skills, and empathy, let's get started.

Using this information

How might an impact-based definition alter your experience of these ideas (or your life)? Could you tolerate the discomfort of looking at how what has happened in your life has impacted you?

Firstly, when you think about the way people describe their experiences, you'll hear them differently. Whether or not you say anything is up to you.

You know, the teen about to go to her first prom who discovers a hangnail, or thinks her hair is out of place—and who's describing it as "SUCH a traaauuuuuma"—but was still together enough to finish dressing, make repairs to her nail bed, welcome her date, and call three friends? Was her life or bodily integrity threatened?

Mmm... probably not. Was there a considerable risk of death? Probably not. Did she feel her sanity threatened? Not likely, although, yes, she was upset, maybe annoyed, anxious, and worried.

If something were so overwhelming that she couldn't speak, was immobilized, or unable to make sense, it was undoubtedly a traumatic event. That's how upsetting something must be.

I recently took a call from a distraught mom whose daughter was being bullied because of her hair—and who was withdrawing more and more. The mom was worried her daughter might harm herself if they couldn't figure out how to help her feel good about herself. As we talked, I helped her explore her daughter's reaction, and she was able to reduce her anxiety enough to recognize her daughter was indeed distressed and that she, the mom, was offended. I helped her create a strategy with her daughter that was effective. She called and thanked me for "talking [them] off the ledge" and recognizing the difference between being upset and traumatized.

Think about the difference between all the synonyms for traumatic.

Synonyms for traumatic	
Hurtful	Harrowing
Shocking	Disturbing
Offensive	Painful
Stressful	Distressing

Now, these **are** synonyms, so you can argue there's no difference. There is. Even though the differences are slight, they matter. Can you put them on a scale? For me, Stressful is different than hurtful—when stress becomes chronically hurtful, hurtful can become traumatic. I can cope during stressful times. But sometimes, if things are painful, I just shut down. I curl up inside of me.

Distressing is stressful to me. Harrowing is frightening and angering, and it is less likely to become something with which I can cope if it persists. Most of these, in milder forms, are not traumatic. Many could become traumatic if they get extreme. Expand the breadth of descriptions and consider your experiences—does your understanding of these states shift? In what way? Stronger or weaker?

What if you think about the criteria that make something traumatic? When you add that (serious threat to life, sanity, bodily integrity), does anything shift? Do any of the synonyms move to less or more traumatic?

When you place these on a continuum—from least to most in each case, you begin to manage your experience of them. Where is the overlap? How does this help you think differently about your experiences?

Can you begin to spread the levels out? Is something distressing more traumatic than something offensive? Have you been able to function when something was distressing? How about when it was shocking? For many people, shocking is closer to incapacitation (one of the requirements for something to be considered traumatic) than distressed.

Can you begin to see how the history of how we've used the word trauma and the history of media's focus may have helped us lump everything together? And if it has, how we blur the lines and add more to our load than necessary in today's times?

For heaven's sake, if something was creepy and not dreadful, reclassify it. And vice versa! Adopting an impact-based definition of trauma means getting a lot friendlier with a wider variety of words and labels for experiences.

After all, why add to your load if you can lighten it a little? It doesn't diminish what happened to you. It allows you to own it as well as to own a variety of other experiences.

Maybe you're in a work setting that has become toxic or painful. The same principles apply. The more you can assess impact against benefit, the easier it is to make choices about what you might change

3

ELASTIC EMOTIONS

Overview

When you develop Elastic Emotions, you can self-regulate. When you do that, manage your emotions—you are in charge of your life—not what has happened to you or who did it.

If you've visited the Trauma-Informed Academy, you've seen (and maybe completed) the video course *The Trouble with Feelings*. If not, check it out! This light, entertaining take on managing feelings is part of the Associative Skills© series. The three skills in the model help you stay connected and reduce the risk of dissociation. Self-regulation is a critical skill in

Emotional Intelligence and something changed by overwhelming, traumatic experiences.

"Self-regulation" is the ability to turn the volume on your feelings up and down in different situations. Managing your emotions this way helps you develop sturdier

friendships, improves your work relationships, and your relationship with you. It's also reparative work for the developmental gaps that overwhelming experiences can cause.

The challenge of exposure to overwhelming childhood experiences is this: when an infant, toddler, or child's brain perceives danger, everything else except physical survival becomes secondary. That includes being able to access existing skills and developing skills in identifying and managing feelings.

Worse yet? If the little one is in a situation where their parents can't help them soothe and help them integrate what's happened, they may develop a stuck spot emotionally.

The stimulus of the memory of what happened may **generalize** (for example, they startle when they hear not just one specific loud noise but **any** loud noise). Similar cues take them right to being stuck in whatever emotion their brains mustered when the first experience happened.

You can see this in rescue pets. I have a very faithful cat—she is older, over 12. When she was a kitten and surrendered to a local cat shop, a young woman adopted her. The young woman became pregnant and gave the nine-month-old kitten to her father.

Her father gave this cat to a neighbor when the cat was about 16 months old. The neighbor wasn't too wild about cats. He brought the young cat back to the shop where she got her. He exclaimed, "This cat is using my floor as a litter box!" (He said it a little more crudely.) He dropped her on the floor and left.

When I decided to add a second cat to my life, I went to the cat shop to deliver papers for their litter. I found a cat sitting on my feet and considered it a sign. After three days of getting to know her, I took her home.

She's been in my home for over ten years, and I have picked her up more in the last two weeks than in her entire life: she's been sick. Katie doesn't like to be approached from above. If you put your hand over her head, palm down, she'll run. She doesn't want to be picked up: she'll hide.

Now that she is getting better from the infection she had, she still gets to a particular place in the house and does a rapid U-turn. That's where I picked her up to put her in her carrier to go to the vet—once. She's still getting comfortable with the fact that I'm not going to dose her with something when I go to feed her in the morning. She hides for about two hours. Every day she comes out a little earlier.

Katie's behavior is a classic example of generalizing what happened in the past to the present. Chances are she'll keep approaching her previous normal quickly because her environment is secure, protected from danger, and I am willing to honor her fear.

About Elastic Emotions

As you read this chapter, you'll learn:

1. About the role emotions and feelings play in life.

2. The impact overwhelming, traumatic experiences have on emotions.

3. How to find opportunities to experience, manage and choose feelings.

4. How to expand the number of feelings you might name, describe, or experience., increasing your emotional literacy.

Here's a secret I'm going to blurt out: you **need** to expand the variety of feelings you experience. And it would be best if you strengthened your positive emotions, all of them.

Please note that this leaves the unhappiness you're accustomed to intact. We each have a certain level of pain or negative feelings we need. We need them at that level to know who we are and how to act in the world. There's no getting rid of them, and you don't want to. These feelings can be helpful, provide a needed perspective—it's important to add balance.

When you strengthen your ability to tolerate some discomfort as well as evoke comfort (positive feelings), the negative ones are less overwhelming or powerful when they occur. It's easier to befriend them and help heal the hurt.

It's important to say that all the individual healing in the world doesn't fix structural and institutionalized systems. Prejudice and hatred against people who are different in some way will probably always exist.

We erode that improper use of power by quietly and definitively strengthening our right use of power. We increase our emotional intelligence and live it. We heal. Our personal use of power with ourselves becomes a social virus.

Suppose you're working with a life coach or a counselor. Good for you! Remember that you need the strength to manage the hard work—and develop more elastic emotions. Most people in pain want to have it stop at once, and often the first work is making sure that the work won't unduly increase your distress. When you act on the knowledge here and just practice repeatedly, change happens.

Why Develop Elastic Emotions?

The goal is to create your own internal "mixing board" for your emotions, one with 50 or 60 different channels (feelings). Like a sound engineer producing a piece of music, you can adjust any of them. You can combine them in different ways.

It helps when you can experience feelings at about the same level everyone else does (at least in public and in the workplace). When something terrible happens to you, your first feelings may be a lot stronger than everyone else's, and that's usual. It's when they stay that way that it becomes troublesome. It's equally problematic if you don't feel anything in the face of something big.

As you're creating your internal 'mixing board,' you're expanding your inner world and gaining mastery over your outer world.

Latrelle called me to talk about work. When she was in design meetings at the architectural firm where she worked, the team passed over every idea she brought up—until a man took it on as his own and introduced it. Then it was "remarkable" or "great work."

She feels stupid and worthless at work. She's making more errors than she'd like to admit, and she's way too grumpy at home. She says she's having nightmares about work. Her boss sounds like a tough person. Unrealistic expectations, ever-shifting deadlines, and a lack of general civility are the norm.

Then the firm won an award for her design that a much younger and less experienced peer had co-opted. That was too much. Latrelle filed a complaint, saying that they were creating a hostile work environment based on race, age, and gender. They turned up the negativity. She's considering quitting. She needs relief, and she says she feels like her brain has been hijacked by what's happening.

Latrelle knows her family was low in emotional literacy. Her people could feel sorrow and conflict, but they didn't know any other names of emotions or feelings except "good" and "bad."

In the absence of any other names for all the feelings **she** had, Latrelle missed out on feelings most people would have in her situation: fear, anxiety, frustration, rage, righteous anger. She only felt numb or conflicted about what to do unless she was shaking like a leaf.

The problem with numbness is that you miss out on all the positive feelings as well. When your brain shuts down because everything is too much, you lose the ability to feel positive **and** negative emotions. It's better to expand your ability to handle both.

When Elastic Emotions start

Infants first begin to learn about feelings as they figure out how to summon their caregivers. Until young children develop language, they can giggle, laugh, cry, croon, frown, scream, thrash, and make facial expressions and gestures. Once out of the womb, infants work to develop communication with us, to relate to us using every communication skill.

As caregivers respond to their distress, infants begin to learn the responses different expressions and gestures evoke. Of course, the way the caregiver responds creates an association between what an infant does and how people respond.

Every day, the break-fix cycle of "I'm hungry," "I'm wet," "I need to know you're there," and "Will you respond when I am in distress?" helps infants learn who they are in the world. This cycle also helps them learn the relationships between feelings and responses in their family and their culture.

Family Challenges to Developing Elastic Emotions

Infants and children are bundles of neediness—and sometimes family challenges can make it hard for caregivers to be "good enough" in their responses. Here are some of the challenges:

Chaos

When there's chaos in the family due to economic crisis, accident or illness, social unrest, civil war, homelessness, family violence, hunger, or other major upheaval, adults who want to be deeply attuned and connected simply may not be able to. Their energy and attention are finite, and survival—food, shelter, and clothing—is the topmost priority. There's no need for attunement if there's no life. These deep connections won't matter a bit—if there's no life.

Kia spent her first few years fleeing war. Her mother saw horrible events, and the militants forced her to escape to a refugee camp. They walked for over a week, with people around them dying along the way. For about a year, they've been living in large tents with many other people. Kia and her mother are the only surviving members of her family.

In families and situations like Kia's, chaos is a constant undertone and exists at low levels. After a while, it becomes the norm, and when it does, our brains do whatever it takes to help us recreate that norm—until we learn to change our normal. When we know what it looks, sounds, and feels like, and practice this life marked by lower and lower levels of chaos until they are no longer part of our energetic pattern, our new normal is more akin to what we want, even when it's unfamiliar.

Think of the people you've known throughout your life. Do you have people in your life you call "drama queens"? There's always something going on in their lives: a breakup, a makeup, crisis at work, or with something in a relationship, their nails, their car, who knows. Their difficulties could fill an encyclopedia.

They're the victim. They insist they're not responsible for what has happened. They seem to be most at ease when they are in the middle of a group of friends listening to every detail. Their challenge? How to create a life of less drama. They need to expand their capacities, those tools that liberate them from lots of personal and professional drama.

When you are aware of Elastic Emotions, profound inner connections, your strengths, and your value, it still takes as much effort as it does to live in peace as it does in chaos. That is, until it becomes internalized and is your new normal. Think of it as a foreign language, complete with a culture.

Lack of caregiver skills

Families where feelings run wild, un-managed, or absent can only teach these same styles to their young. They can only model what they know. Even among diverse cultures, the regulation of feelings is a crucial skill. Different cultures teach it in different ways.

Whatever culture you claim, your adults can only teach what they know—if they grew up with limited skills in elastic emotions, they'd have a tough time helping their young develop them.

Some families believe people shouldn't express their feelings, that it is dangerous to show them. Others have learned to show only an impassive face.

Are you part of a disenfranchised group, of a different race, ethnic or cultural group, or your body is somehow different—perhaps you are neurodiverse or are missing a limb? Or maybe someone who could be hurt or killed for expressing your feelings, or maybe others think your character is flawed? It may be in your best interest to hide your feelings and show only a "flat" face. While culturally proper and lifesaving, neither of these styles helps people learn how to develop elastic emotions in different situations.

Mismatched feelings resulting from repeated trauma

When children have overwhelming experiences repeatedly, their nervous system can become so mixed up that feelings and expressions don't match.

For example, Meemaw and Papaw are taking care of little Joey, who just turned two. He's a cute little boy with a sizeable smear of peanut butter and jam around one corner of his mouth. His jeans are grubby, precisely as they should be at his age.

Joey's Momma is at work, and her parents are helping out. They are all in the TV room in theater-style chairs, recliners with cupholders, and places for the remote. They're up close and right in front of the big-big-screen TV watching a movie.

Joey is on Papaw's lap so he can reach the bowl of popcorn between Meemaw and Papaw. They are watching an action movie, one of their favorites.

Action erupts, with gunfire mowing down everyone in its path. Meemaw and Papaw laugh as they watch the drama between the good guys and the bad guys play out.

Joey is frightened and upset by the killing he sees. But Meemaw and Papaw are laughing as if they enjoy seeing it. They scold Joey for being upset. What has Joey learned about how folks react to seeing people get shot?

If children learn from adults whose feelings are mismatched (too much, too little, or too different from others' feelings in similar situations), these young ones learn the same responses.

Are their Alarm Systems stuck?

If the brain's defense circuitry system is activated repeatedly, it can get stuck—and everything seems dangerous! Unlocking the alarm system and resetting it is crucial.

Children who are repeatedly overwhelmed may lose the ability to turn the volume up and down on their feelings so that their emotions get stronger very unexpectedly, very quickly, and very often. Or they may become silent, symbolically becoming invisible.

A young social worker was sure the little girl was ready to go home. At 18 months, she was "quiet, well-behaved, and presented no difficulty for her caregivers." She'd been brought in after witnessing violence in her home, placed with a foster family, and was difficult to soothe and calm. Now she seemed like the ideal toddler; quiet, self-contained, and easy to be around.

Her supervisor placed the report recommending discharge from the program gently on her desk. It didn't feel right. While it was wonderful to receive a glowing report, she ran through her checklist mentally. She thought about all her courses in child development. "How do 18-month-old toddlers in reasonably safe and healthier environments behave? Are they quiet, well-behaved, and no trouble?" she asked herself. To double-check, she pulled up the Center for Disease Control's online information about infants' developmental milestones.

What she found was that this well-behaved little girl was showing how stuck she was. She was showing how shut down she was by being very still. While she was healing, she still needed more deliberate time and attention to relax and catch up developmentally.

The same is true of adults. My friend Tony is a great example. He had seen combat in Iraq and Afghanistan, and when he came home, he called himself a "human seismograph." If somebody dropped something? He might be under the sofa or glued to the ceiling. And if someone in the neighborhood shot off fireworks? If he were lucky, he could get to the closet before the flash-backs set in, his brain calling up powerful and intense feelings he couldn't manage. There were other powerful reminders in addition to noise.

One day, I saw this in him when I was riding with him to get some soil for a garden. A car cut in front of us, and Tony was instantly livid. I mean, ready to run the guy over! He swore at him and white-knuckled the steering wheel. The veins in his neck were bulging.

Thankfully, Tony didn't run over the car in front of us and calmed that down. It took him about two hours. Because Tony's alarm systems were stuck on alert, everything seemed dangerous. It may have been the driver was from out of town or didn't know the area. All Tony could see was danger and that this driver had done this deliberately. I was surprised the paint didn't peel off the inside of his truck with his swearing.

Truthfully, the chances are meager that the driver woke up that morning and decided to target Tony personally. After all, they'd never met. What do you choose to believe when someone is rude to you when you're driving? Do you snap to judgment and act like Tony? Or do you shrug, give them the benefit of the doubt, and keep going? If your life includes gaslighting, bullying, mistreatment, or other traumatic events to the extent that Tony's story could be yours, find someone who can help you through that as well as engaging the ideas in this book.

Emotional literacy

Another family challenge is emotional literacy. Emotional literacy is about:

1. The size of your vocabulary about feelings and emotions
2. Your skill in recognizing different emotions and
3. Your ability to name and respond to the strength of emotion in most situations in ways that are generally common to others.

In some families, children grow up only knowing "I feel good" and "I feel bad." That's a very narrow range of feelings. If this is the extent of your emotional vocabulary, it's important to expand it. Think about 'mad, sad, glad.' That's an increase of three, and each of those has variations.

The variations on glad, for example, include content, peaceful, serene, happy, joyful, pleased, and more. While each of these is a form of "glad," each is also a separate feeling. How might knowing how each one feels help you? Do they have different types of ranges? Do some share the same cues?

What's the point of strengthening the positive ones? As you enhance them, they occupy more real estate in your head and your heart. This leaves the negative ones you may hold so dear intact. It does help buffer them.

What about the ones we don't know? Sometimes we're a little anxious about things foreign to us. The more we can break those anxiety-provoking feelings into smaller units, the easier it is to manage and master the fear.

Cultural differences exist, too. In some countries, it's impolite or even rude to show any emotion, and there are specific contexts for displaying different emotions.

In others, there may be a narrower range of emotion displayed publicly and a broader range privately. Emotional suppression is common in oppressed people (Black Americans, trafficked children or adults, women who have learned to avoid expressing emotion publicly). The need to monitor and tightly manage emotions in this way might make someone concerned for their sanity, simply because it may not be possible to predict which emotions an oppressor might find offensive when.

For example, in Japan, emotions and feelings are "behind the face." One's potentially unpleasant comments about things at work are suppressed—until the after-hours gathering at an izakaya when people drink and express themselves freely. When the boss is there and says, "Drink and eat as much as you choose!" it's the code for "speak freely."

The next day? Nothing one says anything about what happened the night before. It is as if it did not occur. Some rituals formalize the context in which workers and their managers "let their hair down."

There also may be differences among age groups so that the range of emotions (and when and where they are appropriate) differs for children, young people, adults, and elders. In most cases, children are forgiven for some errors because they do not know the rules yet. They develop skills in learning the rules—and these skills may be interrupted if the children are overwhelmed in some way. However, in the same situation, adults are expected to know better. Children learn and follow the rules.

In **every** culture, the challenge is to think about what you want and how managing your emotions helps you get there (or not!). It's a starting point, even though there's no finish line.

The Difference Between Emotions and Feelings

Dr. Sara McKay (https://drsarahmckay.com/), a neuroscientist who "explains the brain," says, "Emotions play out in the theater of the body. Feelings play out in the theater of the mind." Feelings spark emotions and link to them but are separate from emotions.

Unfortunately, the words "emotions" and "feelings" are used as if they are the same thing!

To make it easier to work with others who don't separate them, we'll do the same—with the knowledge that emotions are neurobiological reactions and feelings are all the things associated with those emotions.

But what is their role?

- **Fear** tells us to pay attention, then to fight or run. Sometimes, to protect us, it can make us immobile.

- **Anger** tries to push away and protect from danger.

- **Happiness** brings people closer.

- **Sadness** tells us we have loved and experienced a loss of that love.

- **Disgust** tells us to back up.

- **Shame** tells us we are invisible or don't matter or that we have done something outside of our group's norms.

Every emotion and feeling brings us valuable information. The challenge is, "Are we willing to listen and explore what feelings bring and what they might mean?" It helps and can make it easier to fit in and become more effective in our relationship with ourselves and others. Both are critical for personal and work success.

Teaching a wider range of feelings to children helps decrease the risk of bullying, trauma, and unhappiness.

Emotions

Emotions are biologically based responses in specific areas of the brain. They are physical and instinctual. Their purpose is to evoke a particular reaction to a particular situation.

Researchers can measure blood flow, brain activity, facial expressions, and body stance against a uniform standard. Yet, emotions are all illogical, irrational, and sometimes unreasonable. All are products of our primitive brain, the one solely focused on survival: the limbic system.

I first saw the maps of where people feel emotions in their bodies in the business magazine, *Fast Company.* Those maps represent the input of more than 500 people of really different cultures. They are like a map of the human experience for everyone instead of for each individual.

Researchers at the Human Emotion System Lab at the University of Turku in Finland created the mapping method. They've expanded the number of emotions researched from 16 to 100, and it appears as if what they are discovering is universal.

You'll find these images when you search "where do people feel emotions in their body." The map can be helpful. How?

First, bring up an image of this work's results. Stick with the one with fewer images as you explore, just to make it easier. There's even a short video available in the Museum of Natural History in Human News titled *Mapping Emotions in the Body* from January 2014.

Find a feeling that you know you experience. Think about where you feel it in your body, where you feel hot or cold, congested, or clear. Is there a resemblance, a "sort of" match? No?

If not, is there a pattern that matches what you feel? Yes? Can you consider that you might need to change the name of your feeling or maybe re-check where you experience it and how it feels?

After all, these seem to be generally universal based on the number of people they've surveyed. If the maps show the places where most people locate feelings in their bodies, working to help yours match more closely is useful.

I struggled with what "normal" was besides a setting on my clothes dryer, and the map makes it a little clearer. It's up to me to decide if following the pattern shown is helpful or not (of course, it also depends on culture, customs, laws, and expectations of acceptance!). On the other hand, they have asked many people independently of others, so there's a higher chance of accurate patterns.

Check it out! See if it helps make sense of some emotions and feelings for you. Remember that you can limit or expand your options. If you insist on extreme emotions in situations others feel are moderate, you may wear out your welcome in those groups. If you can dial them down, you may have more friendships that last longer. You may be more successful at work.

Feelings

Feelings play out in our minds. They are **associations** and **reactions** to emotions. They vary for everyone—they are personal, gotten through experience, and tempered by development.

Our culture (see our book *Claiming Culture,* out mid-2021), the lens we use (see *Changing Lenses*), and every other element we talk about in the Trauma-Responsive System influence what we feel.

For example, you learned what to fear based on your experiences and your epigenetics. In some cultures, and to some people, seeing an emergency services vehicle is terrifying. Others may startle or jump, and still, other people hope everyone will be OK. Some barely notice. Others give thanks that help is on the way.

Often, we can learn to change and choose our feelings to manage difficult situations with less distress. It takes time and practice to become an "athlete of the mind." We can learn to pause between emotion and feeling, and then we can use that pause to consider our response. We help people master that when they take our Change Essentials course to have a guiding model.

What we say is true: "You may not be able to choose the change you face; you **can** choose how you feel." With practice, it does become possible to recognize the feelings are a reaction to some change, and you have more choices about your feelings.

Practicing the associations between events and your emotions (your feelings) repeatedly—practice is the key. It's not about getting rid of the associations you have. It's about adding more. When you have more associations, you have more choices and potentially more balance.

The Challenges to Developing Elastic Emotions

Topsy-turvy early years

How were the first three years of your life? If the adults and significant people around you:

1. Didn't learn how to manage their feelings (maybe their parents didn't know how)

2. Only have two words for the many emotions and feelings we have

3. Have topsy-turvy lives

4. Are unable to be present when children are working out emotions (physical), feelings (mental), associations, and responses

5. Are impaired by alcohol, dementia, drugs, or other biological processes, it's hard for them to be a role model for Elastic Emotions.

They have gaps in learning and skills filled in by whatever makes sense to them. They teach their children what they know. If adults are absent, children make up ways that work for them

What makes sense at one, two, or three should change as a person matures. But it won't if life is topsy-turvy in those early formative years and skill development is spotty, missed, or simply strong reactions to everything.

Feelings that take care of adults' needs

In some families, children only learn feelings that serve the adults—and miss out on the wide range of feelings children need to experience, process, and relish.

As children develop, they learn to express their feelings and how others will respond when they do. This pinball-machine-like process of event > emotion > feeling > reaction > adjustment is typical, healthy, and how children learn. They act, react, and adjust until their actions and reactions allow them to be comfortable enough to survive.

A child threatened or told that they must enjoy hurtful behavior learns unhealthy associations—they come to experience pleasure when most children feel pain.

Experiencing overwhelming events

A third challenge is overwhelming things can happen to a child or an adult. We usually think of negative experiences first, landing on abuse and neglect.

There are so many more: rapid multiple moves, death of a parent, being in an accident, economic crisis, homelessness, over-employed and underpaid, hunger, the impact of parental addiction, medical emergencies, natural disasters, family disasters, financial problems, interpersonal violence and finally we come to abuse and neglect.

The impact doesn't care what the name of the event that caused it is. It only focuses on somehow protecting or preserving the person or proving that the person is not a threat. Remember: there's not always a perpetrator. Sometimes traumatic events are bolts from out of the blue, unexpected, unpredictable, and unannounced.

Overactive or stuck alarm system (adults or children)

A fourth challenge, one we've mentioned earlier, is that sometimes the Alarm System in the brain that goes off when it perceives a threat gets stuck. Getting stuck can happen because of how often the alarm sounds.

When the state of alarm becomes a normal state, the system can go off without warning. This hijacking of your brain is an overreaction and makes life even more challenging.

It can also get **stuck** in this state. Increasing vagus nerve tone is one way to help a hijacked brain get out of the "stuck" state. Meditation is another. Many things help soothe the brain, and learning to manage feelings when life is calm is the best among them. It is as intense as mastering any sport.

Media influence

The final challenge we're naming is the influence of the media. Most people spend a lot of time in front of some device watching videos, regular programming, streaming, or playing games.

The characters in these programs show how people experience and respond to emotions. The problem with this is the operational definition of success and its creation in programming and marketing.

Channels and streaming services identify successful shows based on how many people watch the program, how long they watch, and how often they change the channel. What makes people watch longer? Extremes. This includes violence for violence's sake, violence used to gain power and control, showing acts of intimacy that are usually private, and invoking fear through horror: fights, chases, incredible sequences, explosions, murders, and more.

Children—and adults—live out the models they're exposed to regularly. It all boils down to learning. Learning is lifelong, so that if you want to add other ways of being, you can.

The Goal

Feel what others seem to feel (generally!)

Across the years, it occurred to me that what I wanted was to feel what other people felt in some of the same situations—people that I thought were healthy (or healthier than I believed I was), people whose lives seemed "together" and who were doing well.

I wanted to experience what they experienced in many situations (it looked a lot less expensive in various ways). I at least wanted to have the choice! As other people saw it, my feelings always seemed inappropriate because they were too big or too strong or didn't match the situation.

My goal was good. If I wanted to live and to work around other people, be in longer-term friendships and relationships, or have the inner life of someone who didn't grow up chronically traumatized by all sorts of things? Then I decided it would probably help to be more aligned with the inner lives of the people who succeed at those tasks, emotional role models with high levels of emotional intelligence, as it were.

It makes a significant difference. While there are times when I can still get angry at the drop of a hat, like when I'm hungry, lonely, or tired—anybody recognize that? —most of the time, I'm exercising intrapersonal leadership in managing my feelings. I'm **much** more in charge of my feelings now than I ever have been. My relation-ships are sturdier, and my health better. Elastic Emotions matter!

Emotions and the Body

Freeze... Then fight/flight

I cringe when I hear people talk about fight, flight, and freeze. It's a handy string of verbs we've all heard to describe what happens when our startle response activates. Why do I cringe? I learned only recently that it's out of sequence and incomplete.

The first response that the brain makes when it thinks some-thing terrible is happening is to freeze. This temporary stilling is common: think about rabbits in your yard or deer when you first see them.

Oh, let's go down the path to my backyard to talk about possums. Possums in the U.S. are slow creatures with bare tails and snouts, long snouts. They hiss a lot and eat almost anything. And they consume an incredible number of ticks. In addition to that, they don't see very well. You'll never find a possum galloping like a fox. One interesting fact about possums is that they are the only marsupial in North America!

One night I cut across my back yard to check on a package for a neighbor who was on a trip. I was about halfway there when I heard a loud hiss and saw two big eyes. It was a possum, and we were both surprised. It initially **froze** to figure out what to do—and when it became clear that it couldn't **fight** or take **flight**, it played dead.

After a "no" on fight/flight, that possum's brain decided it had a low risk of survival in the face of an Australian shepherd (I was pet sitting, and that good dog heard the fuss and came out into the yard). What could the possum do? It had two options:

immobility or dissociation. The possum's brain went for paralysis, a form of immobility. Playing dead was that possum's solution to help it stay alive. For some reason, the dog wasn't interested.

The freeze > fight / flight > immobility / dissociation path can be started any time. It can happen when you must make a speech, stand in front of a room, appear on TV, face someone else's stronger emotions, feel your own strong emotions, or do anything that overwhelms your brain.

The "freeze" is a momentary reaction. It's the time when the brain is assessing the available information. Based on what the brain decides, the action is fight or flight. Notice—freeze is **before** fight or flight.

These two—fight or flight—are great if you are a person of size who can maybe outrun the danger or if you have the possibility of fighting off a would-be assailant.

"Fight or flight" are unavailable as options if you are vulnerable because of age (young or old) or size, physical limits (height, weight, abilities, and more), or are in a situation where escape is not possible or too high a risk.

If that's the case, the brain has one last set of "fail-safes" designed to save your life.

And then immobility or dissociation

In those situations (where escape by fighting or fleeing isn't possible), your brain goes to its final options: immobility (different from freezing) or **dissociation.**

If you know animals that "play dead" or know people who faint at the sight of blood, you have seen immobility at work. That's what was going on with the possum. If you hear someone say they were "paralyzed with fear," they're talking about this type of immobility.

If you know people who say, "It was like I was looking at myself while it happened," you've heard one description of dissociation (which is a normal response in many forms). Dissociation can be in part or whole from sensation, knowledge, will, affect, or behavior.

We need to experience our feelings and the information they bring us. Our work is to become sturdy enough to feel them without losing or injuring ourselves and others or retreating into isolation.

Remember: it's important to feel them in ways that are safe enough for you to avoid damaging relationships, losing a job, or getting arrested. In the face of rising feelings, the challenge is to respond to them and help them slow down and dissolve instead of strengthening and concentrating.

Like any other skill, the more you rehearse and practice when you are in a safer situation, the more advantage you have in a riskier one.

Befriending Feelings in Your Body

When I talk about "befriending your feelings," I mean treating them with respect, welcoming them, and expecting yourself to learn from them.

They are here for a reason—far more than to make you miserable. Your feelings are here to help you learn how to live. They can help you know what to approach, what to avoid, and about your preferences. They warn you of danger. They give you lots of information when you treat them as welcome parts of yourself. They long to be noticed and tended to before they hijack your brain.

If you have a name for them, and if you know where you feel them in your body, it's easier to find ways to express them physically. You can help your heart and spirit connect to them more easily.

Tool: Work it out! —Big muscle movement

Big muscle movement. Releasing all the chemicals stored from being upset or traumatized is essential. Besides, large muscle movement feels good—it's a release of emotions. It releases endorphins, stirs your blood, and lightens your heart.

It also helps you get back in your body.

You want to set up a situation where no harm to others is possible. Exercise that releases trauma (or just strong emotions) in a controlled way is so helpful! Here's the process.

1. Name the emotion and feelings you need to release.

2. What happened that caused you to feel these feelings?

3. Where do you feel them in your body? (**Hint**: Search online images for "where do people feel emotions in their bodies").

4. How close are you to being unable to increase and decrease the strengths of your reactions?

As you consider these methods that ask you to express **and** control simultaneously, which of these appeals to you?

Manual labor, like:

○ Chopping   ○ Digging   ○ Sawing

○ Moving   ○ Loading   ○ Mixing

Controlled exercise, like:

○ Rock climbing   ○ Martial arts   ○ Tai chi

○ Pilates   ○ Jumping rope   ○ Walking

Free movement, like:

○ Running   ○ Tennis   ○ Games

○ Functional training   ○ Dancing at a club

Do whichever of these you're willing to do. While you are, pay attention to the feeling you're discharging. Notice how your body feels as you let out your emotions in a deliberate way.

It's not about the activity. It's about the feelings.

Note: This **excludes** boxing, MMA, swordplay, ax throwing, skeet shooting, and anything that has a risk of causing injury to others. Keep a little distance between you and your feelings. Befriend them. They are here to help.

Tool: Build a more extensive vocabulary

More words: improving your vocabulary

Here's where it helps to be curious. You own your mind. Even though others influence it, and you may feel brainwashed by situations, you still own what's in your head. It's your real estate to use as you choose.

It takes practice, repeated practice. It's up to you how much you practice—and remember that your goal is to practice the new skills as often as you practice feeling the old ones: the pain, anger, anguish, and despair.

Increasing your vocabulary isn't about ignoring painful feelings. It's about balance, adding positive ones to help balance the impact of the negative ones or the mismatched ones. As much as you are a "professional athlete" about your difficult experiences, you want to become an "athlete of your mind" with positive ones.

Let's expand your vocabulary.

You'll need access to the internet for this—or a paperback thesaurus—along with Post-It® notes or index cards. You'll end up with three groups of sticky notes or stacks of cards, one for each of the "biggest" feelings.

First, take three note cards and write one word on each card: anger, happiness, or fear.

Now use whatever tool you have—computer, tablet, or smartphone—and go online. Search for synonyms for anger.

How many entries are there for anger? Count them. There are many words for anger! If we explored local and cultural dialects, we'd probably find even more.

So, then, if they're synonyms, what's the difference among them? What's the difference in how strong each feeling is to most people who are doing well? How can you use your curiosity to find out?

Write down five or so that are new words to you for each card. Remember that even skilled helpers may not have a large vocabulary when it comes to words for feelings. We only develop what we learn in our families or along the way. Me? I consider it like the Baskin-Robbins® store! Every emotion has a slightly different meaning and requires a different response.

Making meaning of the new words

So now you have three cards, each with five or so new words. Focus on the most significant, strongest emotions in your initial explorations. How do you make meaning of them in terms of expanding your emotional vocabulary?

Here's what I did.

I looked for two or three people from my contact list that I thought were doing better than I was. They had a lot less drama, a lot more happiness, and managed their feelings well.

I called several of them up and said, "Say, I'm working on a vocabulary project—and I wondered if you might help me out?"

Everybody I called said, "Sure!"

Then I asked them, "So, do you ever feel [insert name of new feeling here]?"

I believe everyone said, "yes." Except for one person who, wisely, said, "I'm not sure. Let me think about it. I just don't know that word."

Then (except for that one time), I asked, "What's going on when you feel [insert word]? Once they told me, I asked, "Where do you feel it in your body? What does it feel like?"

They would give me a description, and I would ask, "And when you feel that, what do you do to change how you feel?"

I always listened. And I set aside answers that were too expensive for me (drinking, using drugs, extreme sports, risk of jail). I took in solutions that promoted inclusion, collaboration, hope, esteem, and respect. These answers increased my feeling of well-being.

I set a goal just for fun. I did one word per person, so maybe I learned two or three new words for feelings each week. I messed around to see if I could approach the feeling and see what it was like, and over time, I felt a lot more able to tolerate and manage different emotions. I also strengthened relationships with important people in my life.

Tool: Build Your Vocabulary

I grew up in a family where I learned there were only two names for everything we felt, "good" and "bad." Do you know how many more names there are for feelings? Even for emotions? It's time to get curious.

You'll need internet access for this Tool. Remember that your public library can access this kind of research if you don't have it independently.

Do this:

1. Write down the word you use the most when you are mad at something or someone (my favorite is "pissed off").

2. Now think about a scale of 0 to 10. 0 means you're not angry at all—10 is the most furious a person can ever get. Where does your word fit on that scale?

3. If you asked your friends to tell you on a scale of 0-10 where the same word fits, you might find it in different places on the scale. (Me? Mine is anywhere from 4-6).

4. Make a note of how strong the word is on that scale. If you ask your friends, write down their numbers too.

5. Access the internet, and search "synonyms for anger." (Why? When you're mad or pissed off or whatever your word is, it's a form of anger, one of the feelings that used to terrify me!).

Learning this method is better than an ice cream store with 50 flavors! There are numerous words for anger, each with a different definition. Each one fits somewhere on your scale.

While your friends or family might put something at a seven that you'd put at a 2, the more words for the feeling you have, the easier it is to tame the feeling that comes with the emotion.

From the list of different words, pick three or four. Use a dictionary and look up their meaning. When you're online, explore how people use these words. For example, find out what the online (or paper) dictionary has to say about "peeved," "annoyed," and "enraged."

Now, find someone you think has a good grip on a broader range of feelings, somebody that has long-term friendships, has been able to achieve their goals, somebody you look up to—someone whom, in your world, it seems like their life is pretty good.

Avoid picking celebrities known for behavior that gets them in trouble or whose extremes are life-threatening. Avoid people who are chronically unable to pay their bills, resolve matters with violence and generally work in ways that don't help them advance their wellbeing.

Tool: Feelings in the body

A 2014 Finnish study conducted by neuroscientist Lauri Nummenmaa, co-authors Riitta Hari, Enrico Glerean, and Jari K. Hietanen mapped how people experienced emotions in their bodies resulted in a set of remarkable maps.

I shared with you that I learned about this study in a business magazine, *Fast Company*. They were talking about something usually confined to the realm of clinical psychology. There's a brief video about it that you can find by looking up "Science Bulletin" Mapping Emotions in the Body."

It's fascinating work. Dr. Lauri Nuumenmaa and his colleagues at the University of Turku interviewed about 700 people, Finnish and Taiwanese. They asked participants to "color the bodily regions whose activity they felt increasing or decreasing while viewing each stimulus." You'll find this in **Bodily maps of emotions**, Lauri Nummenmaa, Enrico Glerean, Riitta Hari, Jari K. Hietanen; Proceedings of the National Academy of Sciences Jan 2014, 111 (2) 646- 51; DOI: 10.1073/pnas.1321664111).

The maps they created show where people feel emotions in their bodies.

The work of these researchers bolsters my case for asking others where they feel things in their bodies. I suspect that the map probably applies to a lot of people. I like to check out their work periodically and see how they've updated it. Yes, sometimes I need to look up a word (or four); curiosity is the point.

Befriend your feelings. Get to know these old friends well enough to learn where you feel them and under what circumstances. Caring for your feelings honors them all (which might make them easier to manage).

Tool: Moving feelings around

Anger. When you feel angry, one of the things you might feel like doing is hitting something or breaking something.

It's true that large muscle activity like wrestling, running, working out, dancing, drumming, yard work—anything that uses the big leg, arm, and core muscles—helps reduce the urge to bite, hit, strike, kick, or otherwise hit someone or break something.

Yelling, or singing loudly, is good, except it can disturb others, making **them** angry or afraid. Find a chorus or a group of people who do shape-note or sacred harp singing. Learn to lament and start a lamenting group.

You can move your feelings around when you befriend them enough to know them without letting them run your life. They are part of you, in your body.

Fear. When you experience some degree of fear (from anxiety to terror), singing, dancing, drumming, or chanting can be soothing. Some people act as if they are huge, oversized, and enraged. Their rage masks their fear, like the Halloween cat with its arched back and big tail. It looks mad and is scared.

Some people shake, laugh, or yawn when they are frightened. Many feel cold and clammy. How does this match or differ from the images of the human body referenced above?

Happiness. When you experience happiness, you may (or may not) smile; you may (or may not) feel warmth in your belly. Only you will know where you experience it—and the map from the Finnish folks is a great way to check things out.

You can move your feelings around when you know what they are when you have positive regard for them. They're stuck when you hate them and refuse to see or relate to them. They are insistent messengers.

Tool: Give Your Body Credit

Now that you have more names for different feelings, it's time to pay attention to your body and how it talks to you.

Here's one way to do that. Think about these questions.

1. When do you get a headache? What's going on? For me and many others, it might be that we need to drink a couple of glasses of water—dehydration is a leading cause of headaches. Or it could be that we need rest. Or it could be stuffed anger.

2. When do you get a bellyache or GI upset (like diarrhea)? Yes, it could be the old pizza or another kind of food, traveler's trot, food poisoning, or a virus. Could it be some variation on fear (another reason to know more words)?

3. When *I* travel to big airports in foreign countries, my belly knots up—I feel uncomfortable and vulnerable (two new feelings words) in strange places and downright frightened.

4. When do you shake, tremble, or sweat? Again, it could be a virus, and many people shake or tremble when they are very frightened or angry (like an 8 or 9 on the 0-10 scale).

   Me? I'm afraid of doctors and police—if I see blue lights behind me? Oh, howdy, I tremble and sweat (even when I haven't done anything wrong)! For me, that's over the top, beyond a ten.

The key to all of these? Observing yourself. Over time, the more you observe yourself, the easier it is to manage the feelings and have more choices about what you feel.

Tool: Pay Attention to Breathing

As kids, we used to play games where we held our breath, or we'd hyperventilate to see how that felt. If you were overwhelmed by things that happened in your childhood, you might have instinctively done two things.

One was to breathe more rapidly and shallowly, and the other was, well, a lot like the first—you may have held your breath, waiting for the other shoe to drop. Both are brain-based, what the brain makes us do when we're scared.

The problem with this reaction is that if you do it often enough, it becomes the way you breathe, even when you're **not** scared. What happens if this becomes your regular breathing pattern?

First, you're telling your brain that you're feeling scared (even when you're not).

Second, it means your lungs aren't getting the exercise they would if your breathing were deep and regular.

Third, your brain responds to shallow fast breathing by changing the level and types of hormones it secretes, which can harm your health over time.

Fourth, your body isn't getting enough oxygen. Your cells need oxygen to help them thrive. Get the picture? Breathing is more than a sign that you're alive; how you breathe is vital to your physical and emotional health.

Breathing deeply and regularly helps you learn to manage (or "regulate") your emotions. This is what it means to have Elastic Emotions.

Tool: Increase How Deeply and Regularly You Breathe

Sing. Even if you sound like a calf bellowing, singing helps move air in and out of your lungs in ways you may not often do. Singing in a choir doesn't require you to believe anything except that a choir community, and the work of singing, helps you breathe more effectively.

Laughter yoga. If you live in an area that has a laughter club, or laughter yoga meetings, they can be beneficial in freeing up breathing.

Swim. Not only is swimming a great exercise, but you must also breathe well to swim well. Not a swimmer? Try water aerobics. You still breathe more effectively.

Meditate. Meditation is all about the breath—breathing in and out and paying attention to your breathing. There are a lot of free apps to help you meditate.

I find the Muse Neurosensing Headband® (choosemuse.com) an excellent investment if you like Assistive Technology and gadgets. It shows how my brain patterns change from use. I like having visual evidence.

Dance. Because it's "big" movement, it helps you breathe more. Even ballroom dancing or waltzing makes your lungs work!

One of my favorite people who teaches a type of breathing that helps re-regulate the vagus nerve is **Wim Hof.** Check out his YouTube 11-minute exercise!

Tool: Install the Positive

Your brain has one job: to ensure your body's survival. Remember this. Why?

Simple. It means you remember the adverse events and emotions more easily and readily than the positive ones. If you remember the painful times, it's easier to avoid them—and this helps ensure your survival.

"NO" is (in many ways) stronger than "YES."

Think about it: how many positive, beautiful, good moments do you remember from today? They've been happening all day... what do you remember?

For me, it's the voice of a woman in the airplane seat a few rows ahead, telling someone she didn't like him touching her. It's the cat yakking up a hairball where I was a guest. It may be the cost of a meal in a foreign country I was just in that was more expensive than I thought it would be. I spend a lot of time anticipating how long the airline might take to unload my baggage. These come first.

What else is there? What's the good stuff I can remember? I slept soundly in a room that was dark and cool. My host's husband cooked me a great breakfast.

One of their two cats decided to visit me. I met an interesting person at the airport and had an enjoyable conversation with my sister. My flight was on time. The flight attendant was pleasant, and the coffee was hot. My cat was happy to see me. The three watermelons in the garden were still there and waiting to be picked.

Here's the deal. It takes 20 seconds to make a new connection in your brain. All those 20 seconds that make up the negative thoughts, feelings, and images?

You can counter them by deliberately focusing on something positive for 20 seconds. Twenty seconds!

That's all it takes. It's different from gratitude: this is deliberately reshaping your brain. I learned this from Dr. Joan Borysenko, who says she learned it... maybe from Brian Hanson? I'm not sure of the origins beyond that, and I am grateful and indebted to everyone who has tested and proven it.

You can accumulate positive thoughts, memories, and images. You can create and strengthen more enjoyable feelings.

These help balance the painful emotions associated with trauma. It includes them instead of judging and resisting them.

Over time, the more positive thoughts, memories, and images become as strong as the painful ones.

By making deliberate choices repeatedly, you add weight to the positive that helps balance things out. What's the benefit of installing the good? It's one of the best ways known to help soften the edges of challenging experiences.

Please notice that this isn't about getting rid of anything; it's about **strengthening the positive.**

Trauma-responsive systems are present-focused and strength-based: identifying the good things that are happening every day and building new brain connections with them—using strengths to insulate against and lessen the past's impact.

The how-to steps:

1. Every night before you go to bed, take stock of the good things that happened during the day (even something as simple as seeing a pretty flower). Pick three of the good moments you find.

2. Focus on each one, reliving it, and remembering how good it felt for 20 seconds. That's all—a total of 60 seconds for all three—it takes less time than the ads on TV.

3. Do it every night. Please make a note about what you recalled and how it felt. Start this note-keeping when you begin this practice and do it for a month—at least.

Tool: Find the Choices

First, quit comparing yourself to others in a way that puts one of you down. Most of us 'drank the Kool-Aid®' the media and culture put in front of us: we decided that we are entitled to a life of only goodness and pleasure and of predictably attainable wealth and position.

We came to believe that we could have it all, right now, the way we want it, instantly—and that something was wrong if we didn't have it all.

We compare ourselves to others, and if we have "less" and they have (in our thinking) "more." We want what they have or our version of their stuff.

We bought into the idea that if we just did the right things, took the correct steps in the proper order that our lives would be as prosperous and happy as the person who is the object of our comparison.

Remember—if we were part of a disenfranchised group, we knew this was possible for others and not for us. We have to climb higher mountains to get half as far.

Buying into these beliefs (entitlement and disenfranchisement) is the cause of a lot of suffering. All I can say is, "Don't drink **that** Kool-Aid®." Fulfill your destiny and choose what you compare (like how you manage your feelings compared to people whose lives are the way you want yours to be).

What we **don't** see when we adopt these beliefs is the individual struggle along the way. The effort required to accomplish these goals is invisible. We can only guess how much farther back a person started because of race, creed, origin, gender, or ability. We see the outcome instead of the process.

Underneath it all, it is hard to believe that we are not in control of everything. We cannot bend every action and intention to our will unless we can control everything. There are inevitably periods of pleasure and pain. It's a both-and instead of an either-or.

Tool: Focus on small choices that you do have.

What can you control? Can you make the sun stop rising and setting? Can you move the clouds in the sky? Can you make a book open and close without touching it? Can you make another person do what you want them to do?

Seldom. And when you do, it may be by using the same kind of manipulation you don't like when it comes your way! It represents two perspectives: it's indirect (and feels like there's less risk), and it's safety-enhancing (the ask may be couched and softened). One colleague on the receiving end called it "slimy."

You may be able to force someone to do something if you are bigger, stronger, have a specific set of skills—and this too is often a misuse of will, abusive, and a form of assault.

However, at work, you rent specific behavior to your employer. In your employment agreement, you agree to perform a particular set of behaviors accompanied by an acceptable frame of reference and attitude. You choose to deliver these actions in a certain way in exchange for money.

Unless a request is for something illegal, unethical, or amoral, fulfilling the requests employers make in the way they prescribe is the contract to which you agreed.

Of course, the law may protect you from specific types of abusive behavior at work, such as discrimination and harassment. It may also offer some protection for particular kinds of disabilities if you can do the essential functions of the job for which someone hired you with accommodations. It can only influence behavior and response to a degree.

Truthfully? If you work at it, you have a better chance of controlling your behavior by recognizing and making different choices. It takes time and practice. It's like learning a sport when you've taught yourself how to play. It will feel awkward, and it takes repeated practice, like developing the right muscles for a particular task.

There are -takes, mis-takes, re-takes, errors, and opportunities galore to practice, and it requires an investment of time and will. Reinforcing positive thoughts, memories, and images all reduce the effort it takes.

You can influence others' choices and decisions, yes. Since you can't control others, or the weather and the natural elements, why keep trying? You'll get more results from working to manage your thoughts, feelings, and actions.

The how-tos:

Get curious about all the choices you have. Here's a list to get you started:

Look in your closet.

- How many shirts or tops are there? If you have more than one, you are making a choice about which one to wear.
- How many pairs of shoes?
- Pants? Skirts? Dresses? Jackets?

Check your morning alarm.

- What time does it wake you?

- Ever snooze it? How many times?

- What about on days off?

- How loud is it?

Think about your toothbrush.

- How much toothpaste do you put on it?

- Which hand do you use to hold it?

- Do you hold it close to the head or close to the other end?

- How long do you brush?

- How fast?

- Which first: upper or lower teeth?

Think about meals.

- What choices are there at meals?

- Start time?

- Food choices?

- How quickly do you eat?

- How much food do you take from a serving dish?

- How much you leave?

- Whether you throw it away or save it?

- Do you chew with your mouth open or closed?

- When do you leave the table?

- Do you remove and clean your dishes?

Consider work.

- Do you leave your house to go to work?

- What is the route by which you arrive at your workplace?

- Are there more routes? How many?

- What causes you to use the route you use?

- When do you leave?

- Why not earlier or later?

- How much time at work do you spend on non-work activities?

Think about walking.

- What is the speed at which you walk?

- How long are your usual steps?

- Your steps when you're in a hurry?

- Do you look up, down, or straight ahead when walking?

- Do you always walk the same path?

All of these are choices, either conscious or unconscious. Become aware of them. We give them away or make them without thinking, which deprives us of our power. We'll never have all the choices unless we live in a world we create, where we make all the rules, and everything always goes our way.

What's true is that one easy way to master the levels of personal power is through this kind of activity. It's part of what children are developing in their "terrible twos" as they learn what choices they can make. They also learn the costs of those choices and, as they mature, become more able to select between consequences based on benefits deliberately.

Some people don't believe that we have choices in the face of change. I think we have a lot more options than we are comfortable seeing. For me, if I have this immense power, why did painful experiences keep happening? It's not quite as simple as it sounds, and it's simpler than it looks.

Tool: Checking for the evidence

How do you know you're strengthening the "managing feelings muscle?" How do you know that you're managing your feelings (instead of either stuffing them or spilling them on everyone else)?

Complete the **Checking for the Evidence** checklist and use it—think of it as a catalog. Do you have one of everything? Even if you do, do you use one of everything?

It makes a difference in managing what has happened in the past and how the future looks.

Use the Checking for the evidence checklist several times a year.

One of the braver ways to use it is to give it to someone who sees you regularly and ask them to check what they see you doing. Of course, you may be disappointed—or awestricken!

This checklist is four sets of ten specific behaviors related to evidence of Elastic Emotions. I compiled them from more than 900 people who provide or receive services. They work in business, too.

There should be some things left blank—none of us could do all these all the time! And there are a lot of "if" items. Practice using some of these techniques, especially when things are going well (to build skills for difficult times!). For each one, consider if it's a "Now" or "Not yet." Skip around as you increase and change the evidence.

#	Can you and do you:	Now	Not yet
1	Tell the story of what is happening when you get upset?	O	O
2.	Use different techniques to self-soothe when you get upset?	O	O
3.	Regulate your breathing to calm and self-soothe?	O	O
4.	Call someone when your feelings are too strong or too big?	O	O
5.	Walk away rather than escalate toxic or angry moments?	O	O
6.	Set a timer and rehearse positive feelings 3x for 60 seconds daily?	O	O
7.	Ask for what you need in a difficult situation?	O	O
8.	Seek reconciliation and forgiveness?	O	O
9.	Laugh easily, just for the sake of laughing?	O	O
10.	Ask for a break when you need to reregulate?	O	O
11.	Use I feel statements to talk about your feelings?	O	O
12.	Use alternatives to cursing, swearing, name-calling, and hitting when upset?	O	O

#	Can you and do you:	Now	Not yet
13.	Recognize how your posture or stance may come across and adjust it?	O	O
14.	Use positive statements to remind yourself that your feelings are temporary?	O	O
15.	Take "time out" of your own accord when things are tense?	O	O
16.	Recognize and name what others seem to be feeling (and that they agree)?	O	O
17.	Check in with yourself to see how you're feeling multiple times a day?	O	O
18.	Get angry without becoming violent?	O	O
19.	Have methods to contain your feelings when you're angry or upset?	O	O
20.	Pay attention to your feelings and use mindfulness to adjust them?	O	O
21.	Respond positively to others' emotions?	O	O
22.	Recognize feelings when you first begin to have them?	O	O
23.	Compliment others, saying pleasant and friendly things to them?	O	O
24.	Change your tone of voice to match your feelings?	O	O

#	Can you and do you:	Now	Not yet
25.	Hear your voice volume accurately and adjust it?	○	○
26.	Step outside and describe your thoughts and feelings?	○	○
27.	Continue to function when stress increases?	○	○
28.	Stay present instead of zoning out when stress escalates?	○	○
29.	Describe where and how specific feelings feel in your body?	○	○
30.	Use a gratitude journal to redirect man, sad, bad to content, neutral or good?	○	○

Check this quarterly. Chances are, your answers will differ from month to month or season to season. You might need to say "Now" or "Not yet." The challenge is to take a snapshot each time—instead of making it cumulative (so you're "racking up points!") or across time.

For example, in January of 2020, my world looked rosy. I could check many of these in January and could have told you real stories about each one. April 2020, not so much. Not so much.

Some of the ones I could do when things were fine had fallen by the wayside. Everything hit the fan, and my business failed in its previous incarnation: I was only training in person, and travel was out. Some of my "Nows" that worked when things were easy became "Not yets" when times got tough!

"Now" and "Not yet" are so much better than letter or number grades. Truthfully? You can do it now or not yet. Letter grading (like A-F, which most of us learn to do) is challenging. The reason I say this is that when students get Fs, they feel like failures. They have nothing left to lose. In systems that need to classify and rank, it's easy to use letter-based grading to increase the pool of losers, which is antithetical to living a life focused on community, shared goals, and norms.

Grading, and forms of comparison, put us against each other. Someone must win; someone must lose. "Now"' and "Not yet" flips that on its head.

You can even have this argument going on amongst yourselves: different parts of you want other things, moods shift, choices change.

This internal argument allows you to practice and change. As you practice a couple of these at a time, check in to see the evidence!

Remember that the more deliberate and conscious your practice, the more neural networks you build. The more you add new habits and reinforce them, the more you expand your power in your own life.

Tool: Feel Your Feelings

We have so little tolerance for uncomfortable feelings. We try everything to escape them, squirm, turn away, walk away—and if we could stay present and touch the rawness of the experience, imagine what we might learn!

Connect with the physical sensation in your body. You can feel these sensations without acting on them.

Feel something uncomfortable? Stay with whatever it is, especially when it's <u>mild</u> discomfort, and say to yourself, "Millions of people all over the world feel this feeling…this feeling of not wanting things to be this way. This is my link with humanity."

Just connect with the idea that this moment is a shared experience all over the world. Look up where people feel emotions in their bodies to see if you can connect a name to the feeling.

Your ability to tolerate discomfort by increasing your awareness and use of connections is about coping with daily living pains and injuries from the past.

However, increasing your capacity through expanding the elasticity of your emotions and befriending them gives you more choices and more power about what you feel, when you feel, and to what extent you can cope more effectively. This reduces the impact of traumatic experiences.

Respect it and honor that it is an integral part of being human.

Consider:

1. Where is it OK to feel your feelings? (The answer isn't "Nowhere" or "It's not.")

2. How can you be kind to your feelings? It may take a while to think this through.

3. What will it take for you to feel your feelings without acting on them?

4. Who do you know that does a pretty good to a great job of "owning" and managing their feelings?

Tool: Stop the blame game

We have a habit of erecting a barrier called blame. We make it stronger by deciding who's "right" and who's "wrong," and then we slather it on like mayo on a tomato sandwich (or your favorite sandwich instead of mine!).

Blame keeps us from communicating genuinely with others. It doesn't require that we name choices. It eliminates naming and accepting bad feelings, the need to work it out physically or do anything different. Blame protects us by pointing at someone else.

It's easier to avoid our pain. When we blame others, we can avoid our fear of what we may lose or may have already lost. It delays grief. It's a standard, ancient, well-perfected device for trying to feel better. If I can make you wrong, I can be right.

Rather than own our pain, we scramble around to find some comfortable ground by putting it on someone else.

Think back on a time when you blamed someone else for something—nothing significant or that resulted in life-threatening responses, something small.

Imagine what it would be like to accept responsibility instead of blaming—just because you can.

Maybe you blame someone in your household for a pair of lost socks. Instead of yelling at them and searching through everything, what would happen if you said, "OK, instead of blaming everyone else, I accept responsibility for this, just because I can."

Then imagine considering the feelings you have about that. For me, I'm embarrassed (I don't know where my socks are), I'm frustrated (I'm wasting time), I wonder if I am losing my mind (how could I keep losing them).

Finally, **without** the blame, look at what you've learned and how you can use it. For me? I invested in a sock organizer so that the "lost" pair is easy to see. I feel better.

Tool: The Victory Cycle

A long time ago, back in the early 1980s, I became aware that I felt bitter, cynical, and hateful most of the time. I was wearing the history of traumatic experiences in my life like a necklace of glittering rage. I **wanted** to be happy; I did. I could logically see that my world was safer than ever, that I didn't need to be like a mad porcupine and skunk rolled into one.

I didn't know how not to be hateful, snarky, and generally mean. It was, simply, self-protection and it very effectively and isolated me from others.

It was as if I carried around a fifty-five-gallon barrel just full of ugly. I had a 55-gallon barrel on the other side, but it seemed empty. Logically, I knew that couldn't be.

There had to have been times in my life when I felt something besides this roiling mess that was eating me up.

The first challenge was whether I was willing to feel other feelings, maybe even positive ones. I felt a lot safer being angry all the time.

The second challenge was what might happen if I was willing to feel them. I feared being flooded, out of control, overwhelmed, and terrorized by my feelings.

Finally, the third challenge was almost athletic. If I could find (or make up) some positive feelings to feel, would I practice enough to balance out the two barrels? I felt like they were a set of scales, one side incredibly heavier than the other.

My emotional "back" strained from the one-sided pull of the barrel, full of pain. I just wanted both barrels to be about equally full, and I wanted to have more choice and control over each.

I had no positive stories to tell myself at first, or I wasn't willing to, or I'd dissociated them, so I made up stories about when I thought people might feel good feelings.

I set only one rule: every feeling had to be positive, non-competitive, and collaborative.

Well, the more I thought about the Eurocentric (OK, United States, White) values I'd taken on from my ancestors, in my DNA and culture, the less I liked them. I didn't care for the competitive, me-first perspective. I didn't like win-lose transactions.

My family thought community was critical. And since it was me and mine, as an adult of consenting age, I could use Indigenous values if I chose to: community, cooperation, collaboration, past - present - future instead of past - present. I did.

Then, you might say, "What's up with 'victory'?" Well, it's the ultimate win-win, like when you were learning to ride your bicycle, and someone had to push you—until you had that exhilarating moment of riding solo. You won. And the person who'd had to push you won, too—they could go back to what they were doing, too. It's not "win-lose."

I decided that I needed ways to remind myself of this new schedule of feelings. I made reminder cards and, when I was traveling, had friends bury them in my bags. When I found the card, I stopped and asked myself three questions.

Since there was a color associated with each day, along with a feeling, I had the "feeling du jour" colored clothing. I went, you might say, overboard trying to embed this process of stopping, checking in, and changing the feeling state—even when I started out feeling good, I still switched to the "feeling du jour."

Six months later, or thereabouts, I went home to visit my family. I had the same lousy haircut, same old glasses, and only the new clothes they had given me for Christmas that year: grey pinwale corduroy pants, new round toe walking heel cowboy boots, a deep purple silk shirt—and a red pigskin jacket.

I was stunned when my mother and stepfather didn't recognize me. I strutted past them twice and finally announced myself.

Six months of practice had created that much shift. I still had my barrel of ugly; I just had another barrel, too. And the outcomes of using the tools in that barrel—the positive one—pleased me.

I was uncomfortable feeling the new feelings I'd learned, and it took a lot of practice for them to become almost second nature.

Since my first effort, I've made over 5,000 Victory Cycle cards available to folks I've trained, and I must tell you, the people who use it rave about it. Just like I did!

We all found that it helped us become more in charge of our lives.

It works for several reasons. You're "installing the good," as I learned it from my dear soul sister Joan Borysenko (who I think said she learned it from Brian Hanson—we all share). You're changing how your brain works directly and positively.

This process lays down new neural networks. You're getting to know the feeling each event you install brings, increasing your self-regulation skills.

You get to feel better when you choose to, which expands your power and choices. It in no way demeans or negates the unpleasant feelings of sadness, anger, despair, or hate—it only increases your options, your choices. Your choices are where your power is.

It may start with "head-work" that begs for "homework," and it leads to "heart-work." It is a different lens, one that translates across cultures.

That's mastery. Maybe you have no identifiable trauma—then it becomes personal and professional development. The process? Change your story, change your life.

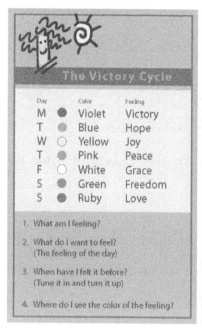

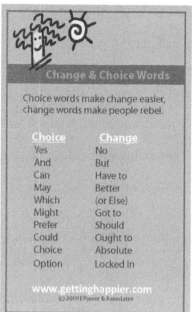

OK, you want this for your pocket, your wallet, whatever you use daily to help you remember to use it. Email me at info@ tiatrs.com to get a printable copy.

I hear you talking to yourself—and saying, "Oh, I can do that! I don't like that feeling, so I'll change it. And if I want a different color on a particular day, well, I'll change that too! It doesn't matter."

Yes. It. Does. Here's why. Consistency and persistence are both foundations of human growth and development. The reason the schedule of colors and days, and feelings works is because it's consistent.

Every day it's the same, and every week it's the same. Your brain finds predictability and consistency comforting. That helps you a lot. Even at the risk of being boring, it's consistent.

There's no mystical or metaphysical meaning assigned to the colors. I picked the ones I liked. It was as simple as that. I wrote the colors so that people who are color-blind could interpret them in their way. Why did I attach the feelings I did in the order I did? Because I could? There's no real reason.

As you use this tool, you might find yourself annoyed some on a Monday, and maybe you hate violet, to boot. The color for Monday is violet. You may want to change the color and not practice because you don't like violet. And you also want to honor your commitment to practice.

When that happens for me, I still use the three questions and one action.

1. What am I feeling?

2. What do I want to feel (the feeling of the day)?

3. Tune it in, turn it up.

4. Look for the color of the day to help anchor the feeling.

Here's how it might sound inside your head at that moment: "I _hate_ purple. Why does today have to have violet for a color? Ok.

"I'm feeling annoyed. I want to feel victory, that win-win thing.

"Now, what story am I going to call up that has that feeling? Right. With violet.

"Wait, I remember my friend helping me catch a fish! She was as excited as I was! OK, let me turn that up..."

And then start to look for anything that is colored violet. Remind yourself the color is an anchor, nothing more, just a visual reminder.

Let me stretch that out a little bit. Maybe it's a month or so later, and it's another Monday.

Sadly, I am annoyed when my alarm goes off, reminding me to check in and use the Victory Cycle. I'm not interested in feeling victory, and I still hate purple. Even more annoying, I enjoy being annoyed on this Monday, and I am not interested in asking the magic questions.

I decided I needed to feel annoyed for five more minutes. Feeling annoyed ought to be as important as feeling good, after all, if every feeling brings me a message or information. It was hard to stay annoyed that long.

You know what? You can do that too. You can feel something, and you can decide how long you want to feel it (almost all the time) before you switch over to the feeling of the day and look for something that matches that day's color. The act of recognizing the feeling (annoyed), accepting it, and giving it room to exist is powerful.

The other version of that is that after you've spent a couple of months using the Victory Cycle as it's written, you've strengthened that "muscle," going from negative-to-positive or positive-to-positive. That strength makes it easier for you to choose different feelings, avoid getting stuck in one, and have more control and choice over your emotions and life.

Tool: Apps and Elastic Emotions

Think about this: the symptoms or adaptive behavior you develop because of trauma don't care about the diagnosis. They just want relief.

It might come as a surprise when I say that you can find some of the best apps for learning about feelings by searching "Social skills" or "autism."

People with autism also grow up with challenges in social skills and often enjoy technology. Be confident in looking for tools in someone else's sandbox. In this matter, use any lane you can find, and recognize that you're borrowing from a field. Play nice.

The symptoms just want relief.

Enjoy looking at and working with apps for younger ages—they might be just what you need. Sometimes it's easier to start with developmental skills from more youthful levels.

In your App Store, whether Android®, Google®, Windows® or iPhone®, check these categories—and try what you find:

Autism. People who are on the spectrum often find emotions challenging. There are lots of helpful apps to help folks name feelings and do something different with them.

Social-Emotional Skills. Self-regulation (having elastic emotions) is a crucial skill in social-emotional skills.

Emotional intelligence. Managing feelings is part of emotional intelligence.

Trauma recovery. See what's in this category, too.

Some are free, and some are cheap. My favorites (valid as of 2020):

Avokiddo

Discovering emotions with Zeely

Emotions Bundle—I Can Do

Breathe, Think, Do with Sesame

Smiling Mind

Moodmeter

Tool: Real people real practice

Change your mind. At some point, you'll *need* to be in relationships with others where you can stretch your emotional muscles, practice managing some feelings, and make different choices to see what happens. Athletes and artists practice and rehearse.

Finding situations that allow you to practice changing your mind with low-risk consequences is essential. Here's where it can help to live somewhere a little bigger. Look up "meet-ups" and see if there's a group you might join—once. Go, and decide to do something else. Thank them, and excuse yourself.

See what it feels like to change your mind. Practice makes it easier.

Finding groups you can enter and leave (because that is an accepted norm in those groups) gives you places to test your skills without "blowing up" your friendships.

Sort your friends. Think about the people you call "friend." Chances are, you could sort them into three or four groups.

There are a lot of friends that I see every year or so. Some I see about twice a year, and there are more groups.

Here's another one: a few people I talk to or see three or four times a year. And another: there are some I see monthly.

Who could I call at 2 AM if the world crashed in on me? Those friends are rare.

Now think about your friends from another perspective—change lenses. From each group, find the people around whom you can experience your feelings freely. Around whom would you express annoyance to anger? Who will sit with you when you are terrified?

They may sort differently than they did the first time.

Use the movies. Films are a great way to set up feelings to manage. I find a tear-jerker when I know I need a good cry (because I am snarky, have a headache, and angry at everything). Or sometimes I need to laugh, so I see a comedy film. Use film to help you feel.

Build sturdy relationships. Slow down the speed of disclosure. Remember, people who have less traumatic childhoods don't lead with harrowing stories; they spend a lot of time talking about other things for a long time before they dish (talk) about their tragedies.

They symbolically make deposits into and withdrawals from an emotional bank account. This account requires reciprocity, a two-way relationship. Constantly redirecting the conversation to your unhappiness, problems, how the boss or company did you wrong, or your traumatic experiences will quickly drive people away.

4

FINDING CONNECTIONS

Overview

You know that warm feeling when you see young puppies or kittens clamoring for their mother's love and food? Or when you see the adoring way new mothers gaze at their child when they first see him or her?

Those profound connections between mothers and their newborns are critical. Most of us call that feeling love—you see the love and care they have for each other, and you feel a little of it too.

When you see that gaze between a mother and her newborn, you witness the beginning of attachment. When you see the very young seeking out their mother, leaving and returning, checking to see if mom is there, especially if they are anxious or upset, you observe the process of attunement.

A trip to the dictionary

Merriam-Webster's dictionary defines attachment in several ways:

A device connected to a machine or implement.

Affectionate regard for an animal, person, place, idea, thing, or concept.

The strong emotional bond between an infant and their caregiver, based on the infant's dependency on the caregiver for food, shelter, support, and care.

The process by which an infant develops the strong emotional bond with their caregiver.

The "process" in the next-to-the-last line to which Merriam Webster refers is attunement. It's a repetitive break-fix process, as the infant learns which adults respond to them (and how) when they are in distress. This distress could be when the infant is wet, hungry, tired, injured, or needs to check in to ensure that the caregiver is still there.

The dictionary defines attunement as "to make aware or responsive." Children work to make their caregivers aware of and responsive to their needs. They practice different sounds and gestures until they find what works.

How do you do this in your adult life? How do you find out what causes other people to respond to you? How do you use that to help yourself in your relationships? How has it changed how others react to you?

What attachment and attunement help us learn

Whether they are four-legged or two-legged, the young come to recognize three things through this process of "break-fix":

1. The degree to which their caregiver will be there for them when times are tough or good.

2. How their caregiver has been there for them is how they should respond to others.

3. How their caregiver has been there for them is how they should respond to themselves.

So, of course, as children grow up, if times are tough in their households, their caregivers may or may not be able to be there for them. When caregivers are overwhelmed, attunement (and, therefore, attachment) may not be so good.

Luisa spends her days as an agricultural worker, working hard to create a better life for her children. Sometimes they pick alongside their mother. Most of the time, they go to the state's migrant education program to educate the children of people who harvest fruits and vegetables.

It's hard because her high-school-age daughter goes to school in as many as three states each school year as they move to pick crops, and the states have different requirements and counted credits differently.

Her newborn? That's a different story. ChiChi (that's his nickname) goes from adult to adult to be cared for during the day.

Luisa is exhausted when she comes home, and after she takes her turn in the camp's showers, eats, and goes to bed. She sometimes falls asleep with Chichi crying on her shoulder.

The family enjoys their community, all of whom travel together on a truck from location to location. While small and cramped, their quarters ring with laughter and music around the fires in the evening. The children play in the shadows, laughing and chattering. They traveled together year to year, working hard in less-than-ideal conditions for low wages with minimal access to healthcare and education.

What about James? His father was a minister, one who used to move every two years like clockwork. They moved out, then the new minister and his (the minister was almost always a man back then) family moved in the same day.

Imagine life for James's mother. For one of the moves, she was pregnant, and James was not yet two. Her pregnancy was difficult and brought with it unrelenting nausea. She had to pack everything they brought with them. Her husband wasn't excited about his next call and felt they were moving to a problematic church.

Between her nausea, packing, and James crying for her attention, she was miserable. She could barely tolerate the heightened stress. The couple was not on the best of terms as a result. She had nothing left over for James. It was all she could do to feed him and keep his pants changed. He cried and reached for her all the time, and all she could do was hold on to the dresser and turn away to pack.

It's important to remember that caregivers may be overwhelmed with family medical crises, military deployment, job loss, and many other events that have no perpetrator. The lack of access to economic opportunities in her home country victimized Luisa's family. James's family was subject to frequent moves with minimal support for his primary caregiver. In both of these, there is no perpetrator we can hate.

Many traumatic experiences have no perpetrator. Many of them can affect attachment when they occur early in a child's life, and there is no relief or recovery from the stressors. The mental health community has a body of knowledge about the problems resulting from lack of or injury to attachment and categorizes those problems as forms of mental illness.

Labeling normal reactions to overwhelming, abnormal events as mental illness does a disservice to people who experience natural disasters, a parent's death, pandemics, and more.

The Trauma-Informed Academy and the Trauma-Responsive System categorize most problems people develop as "adaptations to what has happened." While they were once helpful, they now make daily functioning more difficult and need adjustment. They are learned adaptations that make sense in the context of difficult experiences in childhood. If you are lucky enough to get to adulthood without anything traumatic happening to you, you may experience trauma as an adult. Even then, you may develop adaptive responses to traumatic situations at work, in your relationships, or in the world.

Some people with some difficulties need counseling and therapy. And yet, 80% of the people who experience traumatic events, whether at home or work, don't develop PTSD. And **most** people can reframe their thoughts, practice different behaviors, and increase their emotional literacy—which helps a lot. It takes practice, which is what all the TIA courses and the Trauma-Responsive System (TRS) recognize as necessary.

The TRS sees this work as learning, becoming an "athlete of the mind," as it were. Increasing your Emotional Intelligence using a trauma-responsive lens makes life easier, work better, and relationships sturdier.

Finally, there is a flaw in this work—in many mental health practices, talent, and personal development models. I speak about personal change, improving your skills to master situations. In many cases, distress is embedded in social structures that need to change.

Whatever country you call home, racism, structural violence, sexism, ageism, and more contribute to experiences that are very likely to be processed as traumatic. Society, as a whole, must solve these; your work is to reduce the impact they have on you and your family's future generations. Relationships are required to do this work.

The Five Good Things of Growth-Promoting Relationships

In the 1970s, Jean Baker-Miller began to change the lens shining on relationships. She was a Japanese American woman, a polio survivor, and a psychiatrist when women were rarely MDs, let alone psychiatrists.

She began to talk and write about how many of our challenges were in the connections we have to others. How we connect, navigate changes in relationships, and sustain caring as connections change.

She thought we should focus on what she called "growth-fostering relationships." Growth-fostering relationships have five essential attributes, characteristics that Dr. Baker-Miller called the Five Good Things. The features that mark a growth-fostering relationship are listed below.

1. **Sense of Zest** or **Energy**
2. **Increased Sense of Worth**

3. **Clarity**: Increased knowledge of oneself and the other person in the relationship

4. **Productivity**: Ability and motivation to act both in the relationship and outside of it

5. **A desire for more Connection**: In reaction to the satisfaction of the relational experience

Even if we seek these through <u>negative</u> actions because they have proven effective, these five good things are what people seek in relationships.

If you think about kids, they want this from their caregivers up to a certain age. Then, the fifth item becomes "Change in connection that continues the relationship in another way."

We foster this as inner connections to others, animals, spirituality, places—ways of knowing and remembering even when we are apart.

Connection and how you learn it

There's a saying that "you catch more flies with honey than you do with vinegar." It seems that using skills and tools that help us use "honey" to change how we connect at any level with others, nature, animals, plants, and the universe in which we live might be the way to go. We can always use vinegar.

Chances are, if you have a history of a difficult childhood, you have all the vinegar you need. No matter how your experiences defined "difficult," learning, practicing, and connecting in different ways helps you neutralize your "vinegar." You add skills, knowledge, choices, and power.

These all supplement the process of feeling good in a relationship and remembering that feeling later on when you call the event to mind. It's a stress-relieving, mindfulness-based process.

Recognizing existing connections

Connection is a natural extension of attachment. People say "I have a connection to…" or "let's connect…" or "I feel connected to…" to point out how they are related to something or someone else, usually in a positive way.

Despite my fear of ruptured connections because of my behavior and attitude back then, the people I went to school with—and the school itself—held positive regard and felt connected. I don't need to know how or why; I just need to enjoy it. Now I can think of the school and feel a smile creep across my face.

A few minutes ago, I saw a Facebook post from a friend in a part of New Mexico that one of my adopted families calls home. When I saw the familiar opening of the home east to the sky, I felt a warming in my heart. I thought of my people there who love me.

Then a friend dropped by to show off a new tattoo she'd gotten to commemorate mastery over something. That's a connection, too, because it reminds her of her skill in overcoming.

There are so many ways in which we connect! And they all help us.

Connections and coping

These days, triggers are what we call those firmly embedded negative connections to things that have caused an injury. Our brains may call them up and hijack us unexpectedly. In some places, triggers are switches in software, something you pull to activate a garden hose, or a type of finger problem.

Frankly, if you watch crime shows, action movies, horror, or science fiction flicks, read thrillers, murder mysteries, or other graphically descriptive material, and don't call it triggering, you might want to rethink your threshold. The word trigger has become a trigger.

There are reminders, markers, memories, switches, cues, signals, prompts, and more—all of which may be accompanied by negative emotions, uncomfortable feelings, and discomfort. They fall short of being triggers for flashbacks.

It's all about memory and exposure. When we're triggered, we remember a sight, sound, taste, touch, or smell associated with something that has happened. It is as if we are right there again. Our brain tries to protect us from harm by remembering the threats and calling them up often (and powerfully). If we've forgotten, we could be at risk.

Do we have triggers or reminders for positive or helpful connections? Not as often. Seriously, how often do you have flashbacks about the good things that have happened? Does it even happen? Wait—do you recognize it as of equal strength?

What's the difference between a loud alarm and a trigger? Volume and intensity. But do we call both triggers? Generally, yes. Calling both the same thing makes events worse than they are because alarms need a lesser reaction than triggers. There's usually a continuum for most experiences, and each point on it has a different name—and each point on the scale is different.

Because brains focus on the negative to reduce survival threats, focusing on non-survival feel-good memories is less critical to the brain.

Feel-good memories are <u>not</u> less important to you. They may be <u>more</u> critical because of their role in helping you increase your social and emotional intelligence!

It isn't about giving up the negative or the flashbacks or forgetting what happened that has been so difficult. Honoring the memories of natural disasters, accidents, medical issues, becoming a crime victim, or traumatic experiences in relationships is vital. So is adding more positive memories to the "bank."

It is about adding to the toolkit, strengthening your awareness, and using positive memories (and, yes, there are some) to strengthen yourself against other potential threats to survival.

As you strengthen the positive memories, still addressing the ones that hijack your brain as negative triggers, it's easier for the brain to <u>reduce</u> how often, how much, and how strongly it calls on the negative triggers.

Strengthening inner connections

The first way to strengthen inner connections is to <u>recognize</u> that both positive and negative ones exist. The negative ones are often stronger when you have a history of trauma—because they're how the brain protects us against them happening again.

The positive ones are there, too. Recognizing them, naming them, and rehearsing them makes them stronger. Strengthening the positive helps counterbalance the negative, and it leaves the negative in place, reducing any sense of threat from this process.

Want to have some fun with the positive ones? Go back to Elastic Emotions and find the Tool on "Installing the Good." Look up "neurogenesis" and watch some of the videos about how it only takes 20 seconds to form a new neural circuit. Use the Victory Cycle. Practice!

Tool: Finding connections

Connections help you develop elastic emotions (like calming yourself whenever you're willing to). You have more connections than you think.

Of course, there are many more—keep looking and collect all you can—and use these to help you "install the good." Remember—20 seconds of thinking about and feeling the good creates a new neural circuit.

How are your Inner Connections? 1 of 2

Describe something in each category:

A piece of clothing that is a gift from someone I love:	Jewelry given to me by someone I love or with a special meaning:

This is the story of my favorite tattoo, poster, or item in my home:	These songs or this music make me feel better:
This is my favorite comfort food and the story of how it got there:	Here are a few positive memories of holidays:
These spiritual practices make me feel good:	These are the people whose pictures are always on my cell phone:

Tool: The atlas of connections

Look at this compilation of behaviors from 900-plus people who provide and receive services.

People studying Emotional Intelligence could have generated it, too, because these are also markers of self-awareness, social awareness, and relationships.

As you review these, mark items "Now" when you know it is something you do now. Use the memory of the "Now" to self-soothe and reduce distress.

You can observe and support any of these in others who are friends or clients. You'll have things you can practice that others do to help them identify and use connections.

And by the way, of course you won't check all of them!

#	Can you and do you:	Now	Not yet
1.	Monitor and use information from body states	O	O
2.	Talk about friends, pets, family, others in positive ways	O	O
3.	Call, text, email others and use social networks (Internet, Facebook, Twitter, MySpace, Instagram, WeChat, etc. [2020]).	O	O
4.	Display, keep, share photos of others, favorite places, pets	O	O
5.	Make culturally appropriate eye contact	O	O
6.	Send cards, letters, gifts, flowers, presents, messages	O	O
7.	Gesture with hugs, waving, smiling, reaching out, nodding in agreement	O	O
8.	Listen actively (nodding, allowing others to finish, reflecting without distortion, asking questions)	O	O
9.	Smile, laugh, laugh at yourself and proper situations (humor)	O	O
10.	Cook and eat with others, share food, entertain, dine out	O	O
11.	Help others when others are in need	O	O

#	Can you and do you:	Now	Not yet
12.	Have and use tools, kitchen utensils, furniture, and other items from family/friends who have died	O	O
13.	Make deliberate efforts to develop and sustain relationships	O	O
14.	Engage with your spirituality / religious tradition	O	O
15.	Belong to social networks, groups, clubs, social gatherings	O	O
16.	Remember what matters to others, asks about your interests	O	O
17.	Keep items that have a positive meaning in your life	O	O
18.	Mirror others' body language and lean in, mirror facial expressions	O	O
19.	Plan or take part in celebrations	O	O
20.	Describe events you enjoy or have enjoyed	O	O
21.	Sees out specific events, places, people and returns to them again	O	O
22.	Call someone you care about deeply from time to time or regularly	O	O
23.	Talk about plans that involve others	O	O

#	Can you and do you:	Now	Not yet
24.	Respect others	○	○
25.	Take vacations alone or with others	○	○
26.	Anticipate visits with or from others with pleasure	○	○
27.	Volunteer in special interest groups	○	○
28.	Belong to a sports team, musical group, other special interest groups	○	○
29.	Listen to music or CD that reminds them of someone	○	○
30.	Reach out to touch others on greeting, when they are in pain, and at other proper times	○	○
31.	Use "my" in connection with people, pets, faith, etc.	○	○
32.	Make phone calls to others	○	○
33.	Make and keeps scrapbooks or other commemoratives	○	○
34.	Apologize, work towards forgiveness	○	○
35.	Wear symbols of religion, beliefs, or faith	○	○

#	Can you and do you:	Now	Not yet
36.	Follow through on agreements	O	O
37.	Pay attention to personal space (self and others')	O	O
38.	Defend others in a suitable way	O	O
39.	Share rituals with others (celebrations, traditions, gifts, decorations, etc.)	O	O
40.	Perform acts of kindness for others, volunteer	O	O
41.	Get tattoos of pets, people you hold dear	O	O
42.	Ask about others' families	O	O
43.	Share your feelings and ideas	O	O
44.	Talk about activities shared with others or thinking about those activities	O	O
45.	Talk about lessons (positive and negative) learned from others	O	O
46.	Recognize your biases (judgments) and suspend them	O	O
47.	Prefer a specific recipe or something because of its' connection to a person	O	O

#	Can you and do you:	Now	Not yet
48.	Play music, and talk about your connection to it	O	O
40.	Tell the stories of connections you have to others, places, animals	O	O
50.	Listen to and enjoy good stories from others	O	O

When you call on these in your life and help others master doing the same, you're reducing the opportunity for crises to occur. Remembering and increasing your awareness of these helps insulate you against the impact of tougher times.

➎

REPOSSESSING LIFE

Overview

I f you have a history of trauma—or know people who do—it can sometimes seem as if they no longer own the life they thought they had or could have. Their lives have been taken over by what happened to them.

I was like that. The center of my universe was all the difficult things I'd experienced. It was like wearing a pair of glasses that saw the negative in everything—the "thing" under the bed, at the bottom of the lake, and everywhere else.

It was the only world I thought I knew. The constant fear of being tossed to the ground unexpectedly by a dislocating knee dominated my life. I gave my life away to a past and present that terrorized me. And I let it. I desperately needed to take my life back, to "repossess" it from the trauma.

CreditKarma.com defines car repossession this round-about way:

> "…After your **car** is repossessed, the **credit bureaus** may include a note about the repossession in your **credit reports** for up to seven years… If you still owe money on your **car loan,** the lender might eventually hand over the debt to a **collections agency**."

Let's write that from the perspective of traumatic events:

> "…After you repossess your **life**, the **trauma** that claimed it may include a note about the repossession in your **being** for up to seven years… If you still owe money (unresolved impact) on your **past**, the lender might eventually hand over the debt to a collections agency (your health)."

Some cultures believe that whatever—or whoever—causes or inflicts the injury ends up with a piece of the injured person's soul in the underworld.

In those cultures, people perform versions of "soul retrieval." The rituals help the survivor go down into the underworld and reclaim those broken-off parts from the darkness that took them.

In other cultures, injury is an imposed spiritual injury or oppression. There, the process might be called "deliverance" or "intercessory prayer." In these cultures, people may struggle with inherited, invited, or imposed spiritual oppression.

There may be different frames for the existential losses that can result from overwhelming, traumatic experiences. There may be other ways of remedying them. Rituals, relationships, and rigor all apply to each of the cultures. Repossessing life is about retrieving and inhabiting your life instead of letting the trauma have it.

How repossessing life might look

Here's one way of thinking about this (by the way, this is about *Changing Lenses*). After **wars**, when people return home and rebuild, they are repossessing territory, buildings, things. Their survival requires their "physical repossession" of bringing all of themselves back to their land, their homes, and the people they love. It may be a beacon of hope as they rebuild or restore, repossessing more and more of their lives.

If you are alive in a recently bombed village, the first repossession is food, shelter, and clothing. After that, you can begin to tend to the psychological trauma the experience caused as you move around Maslow's hierarchy of needs. This may or may not be after an armed conflict ends.

Let's say the experience of war or armed conflict is not your experience.

Whatever traumatic experiences you had claimed some part of your life—if they began when you were a child, there may be ways in which your development stalled.

Repossessing life is about growth beyond that point. Overwhelming/ traumatic events steal so much:

- Progressive social-emotional development in some areas long after the injury

- Optimal development of skill in making choices

- The ability to develop healthy trust and self-belief

- Sound sleep, waking feeling refreshed

- Experience with Elastic Emotions or regulation skills

- Awareness of Inner Connections

- Self-soothing skills

- Knowledge of your culture

All the elements in the Trauma-Responsive System, and that thing they become when they are all interconnected in you—not in a straight line, but everything to everything—work to help you increase your wholeness.

Each time you install the good by practicing something you value as an ideal, by working with one of the TRS elements positively, you are repossessing life.

Tool: Jigsaw puzzle

- Go to the local arts and crafts store

- Get or make a blank jigsaw puzzle

- Think about significant areas where life feels impaired by what happened to you

- Create a puzzle piece for each area

- Assemble the puzzle

What might happen if you took a piece and made it the cornerstone of another puzzle, one that you create?

Tool: When you don't possess your life

Whatever the culture of which you're a part believes, the feeling of not owning your life is "like a sort of bankruptcy," as a young woman once described it to me. Another mentioned that she felt like a chunk of Swiss cheese with lots of holes in it.

Traumatic events change lives, steal futures, break promises, and in many ways do take over and claim life as their own. They are, for many people, the center of their lives.

This results in lost hope for a future filled with positive expectations and bright hopes. Dreams are dashed. People feel as their lives have been stolen, dispossessed by their experience.

Consider these:

1. What do you think about most of the time?

2. Was "Trauma" one of the puzzle pieces in the earlier activity?

3. If not, what role does trauma occupy in the puzzle of "you"?

4. What might happen if you added other lenses from which you could choose?

5. How long is it before you begin to talk about bad things that happened to you when you meet someone?

6. How might you add other things to the center of your focus?

Tool: Traumatic events as colonizing forces

At the extreme, traumatic events become a colonizer: they assert illegitimate power gained by coercion; or exertion of power over someone smaller, weaker, less independent (even if only momentarily and whether or not there is a weapon).

The Trauma-Informed Academy and the Trauma-Responsive System know better. We know that traumatic experiences shape and reshape life. We know that there was strength before and a different kind of strength afterward.

Changed isn't "broken."

When trauma causes people to miss a sense of wholeness, this can be remedied.

These are essential questions to think about:

- In what ways do you feel colonized or changed by what happened to you?
- Which (if any) of these feels like "broken"?
- Does it seem like bad things (whether you have a history of them or work with those who do) have coerced you into something you didn't want to become?

The challenge of normal

One challenge is knowing the reality of normal or non-traumatized life. Any number of subtle double standards might exist. What we come to believe may be unrealistic. And it's challenging to find out that you're very much more like than different from others.

Is normal driven by a majority culture or a cultural group struggling to keep power? Is normal good for women? Is it a world that is good for children? A world designed for people with physical limitations or differences is better for everyone. A world focused on collaboration and respect is better for everyone.

What is the basis of your normal? Does "typical" work better than "normal"? Who or what defines you? Is it based on where you fit in with your ancestors? For some, normal depends on who they love or where they live. Others may define normal based on the labels they accept in their lives.

Is "normal" based on things like having a job, having good friends, being cared for by others, caring for others, your health, and creating and managing sturdy relationships? I promise you, these are all fine things to include in your normal. They work in typical, too.

I live among interesting, unique, authentic folks. That's the "normal" I want. I want a box labeled "normal" that is big and open, with room for variation and difference.

Whatever influences your normal drives who you become. How much has trauma taken possession of your life and driven normal? Is your history—whether of being gaslighted at work, surviving a natural disaster, or a childhood filled with chaos—the center of your universe? Do you have other things in your life?

Remember, "normal" is a category that folks who have the power to name, fund, and control create. "Typical" is a word you can adopt for yourself—or perhaps your life has created neurodiversity. The need to be special and unique is vital. However, the need to be special can also toss us into competition with others to vie over who has the most or the worst injuries.

Healing indeed begins when we refuse to accept the defining gaze of the "Other" (people who feel or act as if they have power over us or to whom society has assigned such power). To whom do you give the power to define you? In some cases, it may be safer to accept the definition others want to assign you, and in others, you should probably fight in a way that allows you optimal liberty to refuse it.

In most settings, "normal" is whatever creates the most significant financial gain to the naming party. A more restricted "normal" with a more expansive "abnormal" establishes the possibility of economic increase for people whose economy profits from "abnormal."

For example, a system that relies on privatized healthcare or justice industries needs a steady stream of people with health problems or people accused and convicted of crimes to generate revenue.

When the focus is the economic process—gain-healing and recovery are secondary to earnings and profit, except for those who can set aside the financial challenge. This dynamic changes "normal" and not in a good way.

Repossessing life is about learning the proper use of your power. Affected by traumatic experiences, cultural expectations, and family traditions, power is something we uncover and develop.

We uncover our power as we learn that our "No" impacts situations, helping us gain something. We test to see where else our uncovered power makes a difference.

We develop (through practice) our power to influence, create, choose, focus. Other people whose growing-up years were good enough learned specific skills growing up. People impacted by overwhelming events acquire these as additional skills. It's a muscle anyone can strengthen in the name of Emotional Intelligence, for any reason, to help withstand the challenges life brings.

Tool: Markers of Repossessing Life

When we talk about repossessing life, we mean a life marked by these characteristics, which people develop at different rates across life:

1. Increasing a sense of other things besides trauma as focal points in life

2. Naming, experiencing and expressing a broader range of feelings

3. Deepening awareness of positive connections that offer you inner support

4. Growing awareness of and ability to protect boundaries

5. Emerging and increasing sense of deliberate good

6. Keeping the focus on the present and strengths

7. Expanding compassion for self and all life

8. Developing and sustaining deep respect for all of life

9. Sustaining positive curiosity

These all make dealing with traumatic experiences easier, whether dealing with our own or helping others with theirs. Look for these characteristics and foster them.

Tool: When are we whole?

Frankly, if you believe in two key concepts:

1. Universal exposure. Everyone has seen, heard, or experienced something so overwhelming that they thought death, serious injury, or insanity was close; and

2. Generational trauma (illness, war, colonization, famine, genocide, financial and emotional poverty, and more in

their ancestors' lives) impacts everyone then the next topic to think about might be this:

Is anyone "truly whole," given how broken things are across all our lives?

There are big questions in **this** question, like:

- What does "true" mean—and by whose standards?
- What's the difference between pessimism and realism?
- Isn't wholeness subjective?

Another way to answer this question (for those who have spent years in therapy) is to ask, "How would you know if you're better?" Answering that helps you know the state you desire. You know what "wholeness" looks like for you. Remember, though, that it will and should change as you change!

If we **do** have that sense of wholeness, how can we increase that for ourselves and others—without victimizing others in our worlds?

Think about these questions—you encountered them first earlier in this section. Respond to them.

1. Does anyone have a "true" sense of wholeness, given how broken things are across all our lives?

2. What does "true" mean—and by whose standards?

3. What's the difference between pessimism and realism?

4. Isn't wholeness subjective?

5. If you were "better" from what has happened, how would your life be different?

Tool: Steps to Repossess Life

Check out the Tool on the following pages to begin creating your framework for repossessing your life after trauma. When you look at it, think about working on these issues over time.

Everyone takes time to repossess their life from their past. Creating a new and different future requires change. If you've seen Taking Charge of Change in The Trauma-Informed Academy, you know how that often feels, and you have a frame for choosing to work with it from a different perspective.

Maybe you can affirm every item, perhaps there are some you are still working on, and chances are you're in a different place with each one. That's as it should be.

Your attention and intention, willingness to engage, and willingness to take different actions are the keys. Look at the questions and items below. Which ones are true of you? Rarely? Sometimes? A lot?

Action	Rarely	Some-times	A lot
How often my history holds me hostage.	O	O	O
It's the only thing I want to talk about.	O	O	O
I don't like to be around people who don't have histories of trauma.	O	O	O
If people don't want to hear my story, I don't want to be around them.	O	O	O
I am developing added focus	O	O	O
I spend time where there is no mention of trauma or stories that are about overwhelming events	O	O	O

I spend time in these settings without talking about the difficult experiences I've had

○ Classes   ○ Book clubs   ○ Team sports
○ Other people   ○ Different social   ○ Faith
                     settings   communities
○ Volunteering   ○ Meals   ○ With friends

I can go: ○ a day   ○ a week   ○ a month without
                                   talking about difficult
                                   experiences

This year, I want to learn to:

Here are six things in my life that are "trauma-free" (for example, gardening, cooking, spirituality. These are additional focal points in your life):

1.   2.

3.   4.

5.   6.

Here are two situations in which I choose **not** to talk about my past or present difficult experiences:

1.

2.

I choose this because

___ I don't know the other person well enough

___ I am concerned about how they might judge it

___ they hold power over me, and I could experience painful consequences if I did talk about it.

Role models

Here are the names of four people I admire and who are my role models:

Remember, think about people who have the most freedom and the happiest life imaginable, people who have made a positive difference in this life, and whose lives are relatively free from trauma and crisis. Measure this by your cultural standards.

Check the reasons these people are your role models.

My role models and mentors:

- ○ Are well-liked by others
- ○ Are curious and have a good sense of humor
- ○ Make a lot of money
- ○ Seem like they are happy most of the time
- ○ Can keep calm in situations where I would be furious or terrified
- ○ Have been successful in their work
- ○ Can say "No" and mean it
- ○ Can turn the volume up and down on their feelings
- ○ Have long-lasting friendships
- ○ Create relationships that can withstand the errors they make
- ○ Know the difference between facts and feelings
- ○ Work to respond to facts as well as feeling
- ○ Resolve arguments or disagreements without violence
- ○ Are curious
- ○ Listen to everyone's perspective before choosing their own
- ○ Make a positive difference in the world

Tool: Evidence you are repossessing your life

Please review this and adjust it every couple of months. Enjoy the different choices! Remember, "Now" and "Not yet."

I do this:	Now	Not yet
Cook with family or friends, time together visiting	O	O
Talk about plans, goals, dreams with positive feelings	O	O
Practice good self-care (dental hygiene, grooming, sleep, exercise)	O	O
Eat healthier and healthier (good food)	O	O
Hold hope for a better future	O	O
Ask for help when they don't know something, offers others help	O	O
Make increasingly positive choices	O	O
Smile to affirm my worthiness or someone else's	O	O
Seek new knowledge and skills	O	O
Avoid risky behavior (sex, drugs, speeding, etc.)	O	O
Have goals and ambitions	O	O
Have a job or career suitable for my skills and knowledge	O	O

I do this:	Now	Not yet
Do things for myself and others	O	O
Have a belief system for support or a set of spiritual practices	O	O
Stand up straight instead of slumping	O	O
Participate in discussions and conversations, talks with others	O	O
Care for pet	O	O
Be open about me and others	O	O
Attend to personal issues using the proper levels of care/treatment	O	O
Use positive words and words of connection	O	O
Express interest in things and people	O	O
Work to build and keep positive relationships	O	O
Play and am playful, happy, pleasant mood (generally)	O	O
Think creatively, is curious	O	O
Express preferences	O	O
Express satisfaction, contentment, and pride in accomplishments	O	O
Speak clearly and with confidence	O	O
Laugh easily	O	O
Take care of my health, medical needs	O	O

I do this:	Now	Not yet
Have friends, spend time in constructive social ways with them	O	O
Set a good example for others	O	O
Feel proud of me	O	O
Take vacations solo or with others	O	O
Change my life for me, my children, my families	O	O
Save money for the future and to buy special things	O	O
Appreciative of friendship, nature, activities	O	O
Share food, music, affection, singing, dancing	O	O
Communicate to the best of their ability	O	O
Talk about their life, past experiences in positive ways	O	O
Make eye contact with others when culturally appropriate	O	O
Take time for themselves	O	O
Look for the bright side	O	O
Ask difficult questions	O	O
Give back to others	O	O
Feel needed by others	O	O
Surround myself with beauty	O	O
Celebrate specific occasions	O	O

How can you become aware of these and do more of them?

- Think of it as a trip and select different items as a destination to visit

- Pick a couple of "Not yet" things to do "Now"

- Practice using them even when feelings are OK to practice switching behaviors, which makes it easier to do when in distress

- Give a blank card to a friend or someone you trust. Ask them to fill it out about you and give it back to you. When they do, say thank you and then review it—remember, it's just an observation instead of a judgment!

Check for evidence four times a year and see what's different each time!

6

SPOTLIGHTING STRENGTHS

Overview

When work is trauma-informed, it should be present-focused, strength-based, and collaborative. In many Western cultures, this is challenging: the medical model relies on a system and structure that classifies and rates. In business, we learn to watch our backs because others may covet our success. Events that overwhelm are prone to over-focus on weaknesses, limits, or imposed doubts.

Why is it important to spotlight strengths?

Why on earth would you point out a person's weaknesses? Chances are, they are aware of what's not working, at least some of it.

It's not uncommon for trauma survivors to feel as if they are "damaged goods" or existentially flawed. Something must be "wrong" with them for these things to have happened. They may feel as "everything is their fault."

Many people among your family, friends, co-workers, and neighbors have survived overwhelming, traumatic experiences. Imagine the kind of self-talk the beliefs named above can cause. And imagine the number of times they've heard the same things about "you're such a survivor," "think how strong you are."

In my head, those trite and true phrases rolled off like water off a duck's back. They became meaningless the fifth time I heard them! They sounded stale.

As I began to look for the additional ways I could frame things, my ear perked up when people connected two things: the strength they identified as it related to something that had happened in my life.

Particularly effective, for a while, was hearing "Hmm... I wonder where you learned so much about what you need?" and

"Well, think about it—what might 99% of the people who are not hospitalized for profound disturbances in thinking or experience do? How might they react?

As children? As adults?"

We spotlight strengths in different ways to help build and solidify the person's sturdy relationship with themselves first. As friends, we know that we are all painfully aware of what we're not so good at—focusing on the strengths and looking for the power and choice available to us as we consider our lives.

How are strengths and trauma-informed processes related?

The **medical model** frames the challenges a history of trauma can cause as "biological brain disorders," "mental illnesses," or "diseases." *The Diagnostic Manual of Mental Disorders* has hundreds of pages. These pages contain the names of mental disorders or illnesses and the behavioral patterns that identify them. There is no focus on strengths or assets. There's an under-emphasis on events as causal in terms of adaptations or structural and systemic patterns. It's just the book of labels.

One construct behind the books of labels relates to the payment stream: insurers provide coverage for diagnosing and fixing things safely and quickly with minimal risk. Something must be broken, infected, diseased, injured, or defective under specific circumstances to qualify for coverage. When the problem gets a label, it should be fixable quickly.

This may also be a natural consequence of the mental and behavioral health systems' desire to find a home in the medical field. When it aligned with the medical community, the mental health movement gained credibility and access to payment systems such as health insurance.

In some cases, things that bring us in to care for apparent mental health issues **are** medical (biological—like parasites, infection, inflammation, virus, TBI, CTE, and other pathogen-based processes). These need the care of infectious disease specialists, neurologists, and radiologists to name the cause and determine the care. These people may need psychiatry or behavioral health services to help with symptom management for outdated, adaptive behavior caused by physical issues.

In the medical model, this requires a focus on what's wrong with the person. A "what's wrong" focus is often a merry-go-round of different medications, dosages, and the process of adjustment. It may include dismissiveness from others when you voice concerns about drugs or dosage. The long-term effects of psychiatric medication are essential to consider, as are the challenges of stopping it. Medication—in **most** cases—should be the last resort, and learning the first.

According to Dr. Allen Frances, MD, who helped create the Diagnostic and Statistical Manual for Mental Disorders who said, on CNN (https://www.cnn.com/2018/12/21/health/medical-uncertainty-diagnosis-afm/index.html) that "Mental disorders become the default position to deal with medical uncertainty."

This means that if something is unexplainable medically, be prepared to be tossed over to behavioral health. If you're a woman, you'll be tossed to mental health professionals more frequently than a man. If you're a person of color, LGBTQI, or have a disability, you may be thrown over the wall even more quickly.

In the Trauma-Informed model, there are (at least) two primary differences. An impact-based definition's natural extension assumes universal **exposure** to traumatic events (seeing, hearing, or experiencing). Everyone is affected. It just impacts each of us in different ways.

The second focuses on the impact of traumatic events on learning, earning, and health in context: rather than something to be medicalized, they are natural consequences in need of adjustment. Learning added ways of thinking and being and fills in the developmental gaps caused by traumatic events. When they happen in the present, these skills help insulate us. It can only help us as we do this.

Because this is inherently a developmental learning model, developing a life around and through the injuries of overwhelming events is an ongoing task.

The reparative learning takes practice, with steps to the side here and there, and rekindled challenges mastered in sturdy safer relationships where risk-taking is valued.

We respond to the consequences of what happens to the people around us and to us. We carry the impacts in our lifetime and genetic markers from our ancestors' traumatic experiences.

Trauma-Responsive Systems recognize the usefulness of a learning model aligned with Emotional Intelligence and recognize that the best use of relationship is to help the person have a sturdy place to practice, make errors, survive, and try again.

Trials to success—and repeating the success—vary for everyone. They focus on functioning, on building up the self before doing work that is likely to evoke strong and difficult feelings. You may find as you strengthen yourself that you need to do less work simply because you have expanded your life's functional aspects. The not-so-functional things then have less impact on your life.

What do others care about my strengths?

It depends.

If you're lucky enough to work with healthcare providers (physical and behavioral) who are strength-focused, they will.

They'll recognize that you are more than the difficulties you're experiencing and encourage you to build your strengths.

If you understand how vital your strengths are in getting you here, you'll care. You'll recognize your persistence and your awareness of what's OK and not OK. This knowledge becomes an asset, even if you're still learning more about what to do with them.

Will the "world" care? Not necessarily.

Tool: How do I spotlight my strengths?

Simple. Accept that you don't have to <u>feel</u> the strength to <u>have</u> the strength. This is a place where the feelings and the facts may not match up for a while.

Avoid making up feelings or strutting like a peacock, as these are giveaways to others that you are more focused on your weaknesses and injury. When you do these things, you're behaving in ways that reveal your insecurity.

Isn't that bragging?

In some cultures, talking about what you do well or your strengths is bragging. I think this is wrong thinking.

You can own the fact of something without getting "puffed up." You can agree with someone that you have strengths without making yourself better than others. You can even feel excited or happy now and then when you're feeling your strengths—without bragging about them.

Bragging is when you make yourself look more prominent and someone else smaller. It's a deliberate action of arrogance instead of a statement of humility. It becomes a misuse of will and information.

Pay attention to entertainers and other who brag as part of their process to build themselves up.

Tool: How will you use your strengths?

Start by naming your strengths

No matter what's happened to you, you have strengths. You might be looking at them from a victim-centric perspective, and you still have them.

Use the Secret Strengths Finder. If you want a tune-up, ask a couple of other people to do it for you—their assessment can be valuable. Brave? Ask someone you consider an enemy. You're asking for input, not a vote. You can take all the feedback and incorporate it.

Create an account at authentichappiness.org and complete some of the assessments, especially the VIA Character strength. If you go for counseling, it is more likely that the assessments help diagnose psychopathology (what's wrong with you). You also need to know where your strengths are, which is one of the focal points of the assessments at authentichappiness.org. Our strengths are counterweights for areas that trouble us.

Our survival of overwhelming experiences has created them, along with "good enough" caregiving in early infancy and childhood. Knowing what those strengths are, strengthening them deliberately, and staying conscious of them helps us buffer traumatic experiences.

Take the judgment off facts

Learn to state a fact without a judgment attached to it. The color of the sky is blue. I feel sad. Today is Saturday. These are all simple facts, two of which most people accept as reality.

When you're standing on the earth looking up, the sky is blue—unless it's overcast, cloudy, or colored by sunrise or sunset—the sky is blue.

If you live in a culture that uses the Roman calendar (the one with a seven-day week), people worldwide agree on when "Saturday" is.

Don't stop speaking the way you do—just <u>add</u> this to your tool-box! Try it out. Feel the awkwardness and effort. Work on it until it is just another "codeswitch" (switch languages, as people may do when they get home from work, return to the area where they grew up, or share the same jargon). Over time, it increases awareness of your power just because you are instead of because you do.

Cherish the strengths that you learn you have

When you get feedback (input, not a vote) from others and complete simple, non-pathologizing standardized tests, you probably look different than you think you might.

Argue for your strengths as much as you argue for yourself as a victim or survivor. Take them in with the same devotion you accept your weaknesses.

Tool: Secret Strengths

When traumatic things happen (and even when they don't!), we all do the best we can. And depending on a lot of different factors, some of the ways we adapt become problems—for us or others. Whether at home or work, there are many ways in which our adaptations become "problem behavior" or "symptoms of mental illness."

How can you look at the genuine (and helpful) strengths your experiences developed? Especially the ones that may be a secret to you?

These—the ones below—are the ones the Trauma-Responsive System and The Trauma-Informed Academy see repeatedly. What's your response? How do you rate yourself on these?

Are these true of you? Sometimes? Often? Which ones? To what extent?

1. You know your limits.

2. You're aware of the risks and benefits of different situations.

3. You offer kindness and aid to others.

4. You see more than one way to look at things. \

5. You know what you need.

6. You know what it takes to make you feel happier.

7. You care deeply for others.

8. You care more and more for yourself.

9. You consider risks and consequences.

10. You have a sense of humor.

11. You protect yourself.

12. You're loyal.

13. You "show up."

14. You're supportive of your friends.

15. You remember people who gave comforted you in the past when you are upset.

16. You have photos of friends on a device (mobile phone, tablet, phablet, computer).

17. You're persistent.

18. You have a lot of willpower.

19. You work to make your life better.

20. You feel deeply.

What now? Well, we ask you to read the examples and comments on the following pages. They might be interesting to you—however you rated yourself!

A lot of times, people see everything except their strengths, as others see them. Or they see themselves in a different light. Different cultures and contexts can also change how people interpret these.

As you read the examples, do they—or a version of them—make sense to you? You probably have more of these than you recognize!

Read these, and reconsider:

1. **You know your limits**. OK, so sometimes not, and you're always learning—the fact that you're reading this means that at some point, you said "enough."

2. **You're aware of the risks and benefits**. You're still learning what is risky and what is safer? So is everyone

else—and trauma survivors have extra-long antennae for some things and not others.

3. **You offer kindness and aid to others**. That time you helped someone out. Listened to someone talk who just needed an ear—or maybe helped a pet get up on the couch with you?

4. **You see more than one way to look at things**. There are at least three choices to everything—and you see them all.

5. **You know what you need**. You have changed enough to be **here**. You know when you need to eat. Sleep. Do something different. Leave a situation. Are you still learning? Yes.

6. **You know what it takes to make you feel happier**. See number 5. Also, even though you may use methods that you'd like to change, you know how to make yourself feel different—better or worse.

7. **You care deeply for others**. You have a hard time seeing others get hurt. And you need to know that people

you care about are OK, even if you choose not to show it. There are people you "love" and people you "hate."

8. **You care more and more for yourself.** OK, so sometimes people might say you think it's all about you. You're still learning the balance between not caring at all or caring too much for others or yourself. Who isn't? It takes practice. Here's what's true: you are the most important person you have. Take care of yourself.

9. **You consider risks and consequences.** Sometimes you don't care—and more and more, you're thinking about what something "costs" spiritually, emotionally, physically, and financially. There's always more to learn.

10. **You have a sense of humor.** You laugh easily, make jokes that aren't at the expense of others, and enjoy comedy.

11. **You protect yourself.** You have more choice about when you "let your guard down," which is growth. You recognize you have a lot of power to do so.

12. **You're loyal.** People know they can count on you. You stand up for the people you care about. You believe in the friendships you have.

13. **You "show up."** When you are with others, there's no device screen between you—you're present in the moment, and you'll be there for others.

14. **You're supportive of your friends.** When they're hungry, you share your food. When they need someone to talk to, you make it a point to be there.

15. **You remember people who gave comforted you in the past when you are upset.** Sometimes when you're trying to figure something out or feel sad, you can remember someone in your past who was just there for you before—or a pet you loved, or a spiritual relationship you have—and it helps.

16. **You have photos of friends on a device (mobile phone, tablet, phablet, computer).** You know, if you showed someone your phone, they'd see your favorite people, places, and things. They'd see pictures that make you smile. Videos that make you smile, laugh, and feel better.

17. **You're persistent.** You know how to stick with something to get what you want. You just keep on taking

steps towards your goal. When you decide what you want, you can let go of other things to make it happen. You can be very disciplined in your approach to things.

18. **You have a lot of willpower**. Sometimes you might use your will inconsistently, and you still use it. That's good. You work to make your life better.

19. **You work to make your life better.** There was a time when you knew you had a choice to stay just like you were or to change. You chose to change to create a better life for yourself. You have goals that you pursue. You enjoy learning new things and new skills. You take pleasure in achieving even small goals.

20. **You feel deeply**. Maybe it used to be that most of what you felt deeply was terrible, and you're finding some good feelings now and then. Even more, you are letting yourself feel them as well as the bad ones.

Go back to the 20 questions you marked. Look at them again—do you have more of these strengths than you thought you did? They're your secret strengths that we all forget to recognize.

Change your answers if you need to. Think about how good it is to have these—and there are others you can develop, too. You're an "athlete" whose sport is developing your personal skills just because you can. The more skills you have, the greater your choices about your life.

7

MAKE SMALL CHANGES, CREATE BIG RESULTS

You've come this far. You've read this much, and hopefully, you've adopted one or two changes, and that's great. Even if you're spending time reflecting on what you've read, thinking you might try it, that's great.

Of course, whatever change you choose to try will feel awkward and uncomfortable at first, and it's easy to stop practicing when it does. Just recognize the discomfort, be kind to it, and keep going.

It takes time to get accustomed to life with fewer crises. I know! Living a calmer life is unusual in turbulent times, whether the turbulence is the consequence of things that happened long ago or in the recent past. If it's what you know, what's familiar, and even comfortable (only because you spend so much time with it), you'll do what it takes to keep that level going, sad to say.

What I suggest is that you learn, change, and grow. It's uncomfortable. And you'll probably tolerate the discomfort more quickly than the ongoing torment of being stuck in "trauma drama," feelings like others have it in for you, and becoming a chronic victim (again, believe me, I know).

You may belong to a group systematically excluded or oppressed: someone who is different in origin, physiology, or character. This includes Native Americans, Blacks, Asians, Latinx, people from Arabic countries, short, tall, thin, overweight, and people with visible disabilities.

Finally, you may be someone who has a diagnosis of mental illness, a criminal record, is plagued by a past of horrors, or is believed to be a chronic liar. You might be of a different religious tradition. In any of these cases, mastering the skills in this book helps you in multiple ways.

Imagine the feelings it caused for others who saw me stretch myself and manage my feelings instead of getting upset. There were no buttons they could push.

Sometimes I would weep quietly by myself, but that weeping was not the same as being hijacked by events in the present. It became easier to look at traumatic events in my past with less distress. They began to hold less power. The more feelings I knew, and the easier it was to turn the volume up and down, the less I was at the mercy of them.

Remember my out-of-balance scales, where one side has a fifty-five barrel gallon of misery that is full, and the other is a barrel of the same size that's nearly empty?

I used The Victory Cycle to help me start filling it up. I installed the good to help. I looked everywhere for positive connections, using reminders all around my home so that everything has a story—a good one. Sometimes it felt like I was doing it out of spite to prove I could.

Little choice on little choice, they all added up. Counseling helped, and I still had a lot of work to do outside the counseling office. I was practicing these; making little choice after little choice was the most important thing I did. It was the changing of my story that changed my life.

Consider the events in your life with a higher likelihood of being processed as traumatic by your brain. There are many places where your brain may have been overwhelmed.

It may help make sense of some of the learning gaps in life for some people, as it did for me. I reasoned that if I was busy trying to manage the things I checked, I might well have been too busy to learn critical tasks for that age and stage. Research about the impact of being overwhelmed supports that.

As I kept practicing these same skills, filling in the gaps, the benefits stacked up. I replaced the deficits with skills and knowledge aligned with Emotional Intelligence's EQ measures and good mental health. Life got better and better.

Yours can get better too.

APPENDICES

Secret Strengths

- When you hear yourself use these kinds of statements or know these are true about you, you're finding your Secret Strengths.

- The Statements

- People say I'm "such a survivor" and tell me how "strong" I am.

- I keep people at a distance until I get to know them.

- I've let people in my space without knowing it.

- I know that things will always change.

- People tell me I'm funny.

- When I go visit, I know others change their behavior to accommodate me as a guest.

- When I'm getting upset, I can usually calm myself before I get upset.

- When something is bad for me or causing me trouble, I walk away from it.

- I enjoy getting advice without an agenda when I am considering something.

- I know the limits of what I can tolerate in terms of negativity/positivity.

- When people call me and need help, I go to them and do what I can.

- I can usually figure out what's happening when people are upset.

- I am curious about how others think, feel, and believe.

- I know that I am only responsible for my actions and no one else's.

Elastic Emotions: Self-regulation

- How true are these for you? Strengthen these practices to increase your ability to manage your feelings.

- The Practices

- I make myself happier by looking for good things

- When I feel annoyed, I know I am on my way to being angry

- Sometimes when I feel sad, I find a sad movie and cry as I watch it

- I like to laugh out loud

- When I feel anxious, I can increase and decrease it with breathing

- Sometimes when I am terrified, I think about people who love me

- I can respond to being mildly irritated without going postal

- Sometimes when I feel annoyed, I smile and walk away, and breathe

- I know the names of at least 15 different feelings

- I don't recognize how others manage their feelings

- I walk or move when I am upset

- My family only felt mad, glad, or sad

- I have a wide range of emotions that I can turn up or down

- People tell me I make them feel calm and at peace

- My family expressed a lot of negative emotions

Finding connections: Inner connections / attachment

We are wired for relationships. At some level, we are connected to everyone and everything around us. We see this as we begin to look at connections we have and how they relate to each other.

It's easy to increase your awareness of connections that can be self-soothing, like these.

Soothing Connections to Focus on:

- I can name three favorite foods from earlier in my life.

- I can name three favorite songs I learned from people I loved.

- When I see pets or animals, I remember a pet I had and loved.

- Certain songs make me smile because of the good memories around them.

- When I see images of places I've been to on vacation, I feel warm inside.

- Sometimes I think I see someone I love and miss on a busy street.

- I have the recipes for three of my families' favorite foods.

- If you looked at my cell phone, you'd see pictures of people I like.

- I have tattoos or ink to commemorate events like birth, death, and love.

- I keep old "love" notes and kind words.

- I have clothing given to me by people who care for or love me.

- I wear jewelry that people who love me have given to me.

- Certain smells remind me of happier people or places I miss.

- People tell me I remind them of someone, and it makes me feel good.

Opening Communication: Relationships

Communication skills make building sturdy relationships easier. It's also important to be flexible about using them. The items below are practices that help you build drama-free, sturdy relationships. Master them!

Best Practices in Communication

I can describe "social conversation" and its boundaries.

I prefer deferring and being polite over making a scene.

I practice saying "no" in front of a mirror to be able to say it.

I am comfortable making choices about where to go and what to do.

If I have no preference about what to do, where to eat, etc., I say so.

I like to use language that deliberately connects and strengthens.

I am aware of how language and speech can be triggering, whether I am talking to myself or others or others speaking to me.

It's easy for me to agree with everyone about almost everything.

I increasingly use yes, and instead of no, but.

I deliberately remember that we are all doing the best we can.

When I check for understanding, I repeat what I think I've heard them say.

Repossessing Life

1. Even though I have been victimized in life, I am not a victim.

2. Over time, I have felt the impact of traumatic experiences I've had lessen.

3. I practice new skills that help me live more fully.

4. I believe in myself more and more.

5. The choices I am making for my better life are stacking up.

6. My challenge is to keep making little choices.

7. I learn new ways of doing and being

Sustaining Vitality: Body, Mind, Spirit

Taking care of all of you is crucial. Periodically, see how you're doing against these standards that focus on body, mind, and spirit. How are you doing with these?!

I eat at least three small meals a day, usually 5.

1. I drink 60-100 ounces of water daily.

2. I exercise for at least 2 hours a week.

3. I take time away from technology each week.

4. I take care of my health, seeing a doctor when I need to.

5. When I feel sick or tired, I take care of myself.

6. I sleep between 6-8 hours a night.

7. I sleep deeply and soundly.

If this book is helpful to you, tell your friends about it!

If you already know that you want to take the next step, go to elizabethpower.com, click Get Started, apply, and schedule a call.

We are happy to provide coaching, training, and events to a select group of people ready to change their lives.

AUTHOR'S NOTE

arrived in Nashville, TN, in 1979. I was broke, running, and terrified. I looked for work and ended up a cobbler in the shop that fixed the stars' shoes and Nashville's glitterati.

As a patcher, my job was to take those shoes the puppy chewed, make them look new again, and alter shoes and boots like a tailor for leather goods. The shop's clients included elected officials, musicians, people who have become very famous on TV, and many more. Sadly, the owner had issues with paying his taxes, and the shop closed without notice.

In the years between that closure and getting a contract with the brand-new GM Saturn plant to do instructional design, I worked in public welfare (as it was then called), couch surfed, and did any job that I could get. I was acting like—and was—profoundly gifted and a survivor of chronic overwhelming experiences. The marks of my history were evident to anyone who recognized them.

They were evident enough that a wise Social Worker I engaged for counseling slapped the diagnosis of PTSD on my forehead as soon as it hit the books. Although it was the method of the times, it translated the impact of what had happened and its consequences to something considered then (and now) a mental illness.

Despite that label (and later what used to be called Multiple Personality Disorder), I earned a Master's in Education from Vanderbilt (on a scholarship as a Teaching Assistant). I became a force to reckon with in evidence-informed adult learning and multidisciplinary thinking about issues of stigma, culture, processes, and trauma-informed thinking. I consider information from education, sociology, organization development, cognitive science, religions, anthropology, psychology, and futurism. Critical thinking weaves them together.

As a crackerjack instructional designer, I developed the early versions of replication manuals for evidence-based treatments. I designed hundreds of training programs in the corporate world as well. For over a decade, my firm delivered Risking Connection® as an authorized Sidran Institute provider, aligning instructional processes with best practices in adult learning. I've also given my work, the basis of this series, on every continent. I'm an Adjunct Instructor in Psychiatry at Georgetown University Medical Center. The work I do at Georgetown, and The Trauma-Informed Academy helped Japan develop a trauma-informed care model.

My original training is as a poet at the University of North Carolina School of the Arts. I earned a degree in Sociology with minors in Religious Studies and Women's Studies. Then I ended up with a Master's in Education in Human Resources Development, and true to my genes, people say that I am a naturally gifted educator. I have over 20 publications of different sorts and multiple awards for my work in helping people heal.

All that's impressive. I know.

What you **really** want to know is that I'm a fabulous cook whose kitchen is almost always open when people need a bite, a gifted gardener, and lover of the soil. I live by traditional values and methods that are indigenous or Afrocentric.

I am as in love with the soil and all the creatures (well, except maybe yellow jackets!) it feeds and houses as I am with the bounty it grows. Every plant, plot, and bed tells a story across the seasons.

My relationships with others, and the community they build, are sacred to me. As a human, I am meant to be in relationship with others. I am wired for connection, and I cherish it. I also love time alone to recharge and reinvigorate.

My work is simple: I reduce the time, trauma, and costs of healing for everyone. As a result, I help future generations by assisting current generations. The methods I use are talent development, personal and professional growth, and transformational processes. The work I do fosters connection, care, and growth.

Over the years, I've used and taught everything I've developed in this series of books. I'm grateful for the learning and for all the people who influenced me along the way.

Keep watching. Keep practicing. There's more.

Elizabeth Power, M.Ed.

Made in the USA
Coppell, TX
27 June 2021